Men of the Old Testament

Rolf Rendtorff

Men of the Old Testament

SCM PRESS LTD

Translated by Frank Clarke from the German
Väter, Könige, Propheten: Gestalten des Alten Testaments
(Kreuz-Verlag, Stuttgart and Berlin, 1967)

S B N 334 00474 8

First published in English 1968
by SCM Press Ltd
56 Bloomsbury Street London WC1

© *SCM Press Ltd 1968*

Printed in Great Britain by
Northumberland Press Ltd
Gateshead

CONTENTS

INTRODUCTION

It is in the lives of human beings that we can see the making of history. It is they who attract our interest, and make us conscious of particular happenings and whole epochs. It often happens that historical contexts retreat into insignificance, and coalesce, in retrospect, in one single figure, in which, as in a prism, the rays of a whole epoch are gathered. That is what has happened with the history of the people of Israel in Old Testament times. There are certain names that stick in one's memory, certain figures whose experiences and destinies have remained stamped on our recollections ever since our childhood, with the help of biblical pictures painted by great artists – and some less great. But what kind of history is it? What place have those figures in their context? And how is that history related to our present historical situation?

In the following chapters we shall try to consider these questions, and to show both the history of the people of Israel as it is illustrated in the lives of individuals, and the place of those individuals in their historical setting. We wish to keep continually in mind, too, the question of the connection between that history and our present historical situation. For we do not read the Old Testament simply as a book that belongs to the past; on the contrary, it is an essential part of our Bible, and so this question is bound to arise time and again.

Of course, we must not be over-hasty in emphasizing our interest in the present significance of the men of the Old Testament. If we do, it will be only too easy to read into the biblical texts nothing but our own questions and problems before we have really understood what the issues of the time were. And if we are too anxious to regard those people as our contemporaries, we shall no longer be able to gain fresh understanding of them and through them.

If we now try to get a picture of the individual figures of the Old Testament, it appears quite soon that that picture may take on quite different aspects, even in the Old Testament itself. If we begin by simply asking what we can find out about these various people, about their life and work and their importance for their own immediate present, we shall often fail to grasp what is most essential in the picture that the Old Testament gives of them. For the men of the earlier times in particular – Abraham and Moses – as well as David and others, have meant much more to succeeding generations and centuries than could be expressed merely by a narrative of their own time. So we must always inquire further into the results that their lives produced, into their importance for later times, and into the picture that was drawn of them. In so doing, we shall see in many cases, even in the Old Testament, a distinct history of the picture of the individual figures.

This means, of course, that the importance of the Old Testament figures goes beyond what we learn of their life and work in point of history or biography. And this is where we find that there are great differences between men who lived at different times and in different spheres of life. With some of them, as for example the kings of Israel and Judah, precise historical data are available; we can ascertain the dates of their reign, and in many cases those of their birth and death; and we also have a comparatively clear picture of the happenings of their time. With others, as for example the prophets, although we can often state fairly accurately the time when they lived and worked, we know little or nothing of their personal life and fortunes. That is because the sources of our information are so varied. For the reigns of kings we have reliable historical traditions available, sometimes even official records from royal archives, or extracts from them. In the case of the prophets, on the other hand, the focus of interest in the transmission was mainly on what they said, and the circumstances of their life were mentioned only occasionally in connection with their words.

For the time before the kings the situation as to sources is different again. It was not till after the institution of the monarchy that there was any historical writing in the real sense in Israel – and even that was some five hundred years before the Greek historian Herodotus, who has been called the father of history. For earlier times, therefore, we have to judge the sources differently, and apply other standards in drawing historical inference from their accounts. The interest of those older sources is not mainly directed towards presenting events in their contexts; it is the people taking part in the action who are in the limelight. But here it is not so much a question of reporting facts about their lives as of handing on a well-defined picture of them. But in this transmission from one generation to another – and for a long time it was certainly only an oral transmission – the picture of the individual figures repeatedly changed. For each generation stressed those particular features that it felt to be of special importance; other things were pushed into the background, and new features were added to the narrative. In many cases, therefore, it is no longer possible to say how things 'really' stood, simply because it was not from this point of view that the traditions originated.

Scholarly research is bound to make every effort to take into account the historical contexts of the earlier period of Israel's history. But any success here will be only fragmentary, and moreover, we shall never be able to claim absolute validity for the results. Methods of research change, and this involves a change, too, in the way that we look at those texts that precede really historical writing, and in the historical inferences that we draw from them. Some scholars have not always taken account of this limited validity of their findings; and it is certain that among those of former generations there prevailed too great a scepticism as to the possibility of drawing historical inferences from those traditions. In more recent times certain changes in research have taken place at this point.

This, however, by no means implies that we have given up all hope of any genuine insight into the nature of the traditions that originated in the early days of Israel. The fact remains that here we are not dealing with historical writing of the kind that we have had from the time of the institution of the monarchy, still less of the kind that we know today. Nor can this be changed by the constantly recurring attitude of protest against scholarly biblical research. The demand that everything that is handed down to us in the Old Testament must be regarded as historically accurate misunderstands the nature of biblical tradition; indeed, it applies, often unconsciously, to the Bible the yardstick of present-day historical thinking which we owe to the Age of Enlightenment. It ignores the fact that it was no part of those texts' purpose to answer the questions that we put to them today from the angle of our own historical thinking; and so it steers clear of the task of investigating the essential nature of the texts, and of not asking them questions that are outside their province. A great deal of controversy between the exponents of different views could be avoided if in this respect people agreed to understand the texts from the point of view of the situation existing when they were written.

*   *   *

In the following portrayal of Old Testament figures we shall, as far as possible, have regard to the special nature of the sources. As to the earlier figures, regarding whom we now have no Old Testament historical texts, but who left a deep impress on succeeding generations, we shall deal particularly with that impress, and with the picture of those figures as it emerged in the course of history. On the other hand, in the case of kings and other figures for whom the sources make it feasible, greater stress will be laid on the historical context. Lastly, in the case of the prophets, and in a different way the authors of the Psalms and the Book of Job, our main effort will be to construct from their words as they have been handed down to us an account of their thought and message. We may thus be able to see the men of the Old Testament within the framework of their own history

10

whose imprint they received and in their turn handed on. At the same time we may also be able to learn something of the nature of the relevant texts; for our aim is not to detach these figures from the Old Testament, but to learn through them to understand the Old Testament better.

The age of the 'patriarchs' is that of the great nomadic wanderings that took place repeatedly between 2000 and 1000 BC in the region of the Arabian Peninsula. It probably extended over a fairly long period, perhaps several centuries, and its dates cannot be fixed with any certainty. Some scholars would put the patriarchs in about the fourteenth century BC, whereas others put them earlier, between 1500 BC.

Abraham

At the beginning of Israel's history stands the figure of Abraham. He is plainly and simply the father – not simply the father of the next generations, Isaac and Jacob; even centuries later the Israelites call him simply 'our father Abraham'. It is no accident that this first great figure in Israel's history is designated 'father'. The people of Israel have always been specially and insistently conscious of their own history, and in that consciousness they have always had special regard to the beginning of their history, to its origin, and to the fundamental and definitive events of the earliest period. For that reason, the figures of that time took on a special importance, and among them Abraham is the first, the father. He is often named together with the other figures of that early time, Isaac and Jacob, and they are referred to in common as the 'fathers'; and sometimes the term 'father' is extended to the generations that experienced the decisive events in the beginnings of Israel's history but again and again Abraham emerges from the group as the one who is in the true sense the father of Israel.

But Abraham was not only father in the genealogical sense, the one with whom it all began. He is father in a much wider sense: he was the model and example who showed how Israel was to live before God and with God. At God's command he set out for the unknown land of promise; he is the model of trust and faith in God's promise, hoping when there was nothing left to hope for; he listened to God's voice and carried out what God commissioned him to do. He is therefore called God's 'servant', a title that is often meant, in the Old Testament, to indicate the nearness of the servant to his master, and is therefore an honourable title; indeed, he is even called God's friend. Thus Abraham, with whom Israel's history begins, is at the same time the great example for the following generations and centuries. But – who was this Abraham? Was he really a man of flesh and blood, on whom Israel heaped all those honourable titles? Or was he only a kind of symbolic figure, in whom later generations depicted their own ideals?

Old Testament scholars have in recent times concerned themselves again and again with this question. Earlier generations of scholars thought that there was no historical figure behind it all, but that the narratives of Abraham and the other fathers simply reflected the history of the Israelite tribes in their earlier times and the experiences and hopes of later generations. But meanwhile research has come to a new understanding of Abraham and the other patriarchal figures. Above all we have learnt to have regard to a basic feature in the narratives of the fathers: they are constantly presented to us as men who do not live in houses as settled inhabitants of one country, but who live in tents and often move from one place to another. It is in keeping with this that they are not farmers, but owners of large herds and flocks, and that their real occupation is the care and breeding of their animals. So the patriarchs were nomads, or, as we should now say, bedouin. This characteristic has been quite clearly preserved in the history of the patriarchs, and the fact that they had not yet settled in the land can be seen in their being repeatedly referred to as 'strangers' in the land.

To this we must add a further important element. When God is mentioned in the narratives of the patriarchs, he is often referred to as the 'God of the fathers', whether in conjunction with the names of the individual fathers as the 'God of Abraham', 'God of Isaac', 'God of Jacob', or simply as the 'God of my father', or inclusively as the 'God of our fathers'. From this designation of God we can recognize a certain form of the worship of God among the tribes that had not yet settled. They referred to the god whom they worshipped, not by a definite name, but as the god who had appeared to their ancestors, whose posterity had therefore come to worship that god. We see here an intimate connection between membership of a given human community and the worship of a particular god; but that again is a characteristic feature of the life of nomadic groups. For the gods of the settled inhabitants of a country are generally linked with particular places where people worship them. But a link with a place is impossible for nomadic groups, as, of course, they are constantly changing their pasture-lands. Instead, their god is the god of a certain human community, who is supposed to move about with his worshippers, going with them and protecting them on their journeys. One might say that this form of the worship of God has a more personal character.

The recognition of these facts in recent research makes it possible to give a new answer to the question 'Who was Abraham?' We can discern in Abraham, and likewise in the other patriarchal figures, the ancestors of nomadic groups of this kind, and those groups derive their history and their worship of God from their ancestors. They regard themselves as being in the patriarchal succession, and so they keep alive the memory of the patriarchs. Thus we may say that Abraham, Isaac, and Jacob certainly did exist as persons. We can regard the patriarchs as historical figures who were tribal chiefs of the time before Israel settled in one country, and who were of great importance for the origin of Israel's religion.

When the Israelites settled in the country that they called the 'land of Canaan', they took with them into their new homeland the remembrance of their fathers and the traditions relating to them. And through this the fathers themselves acquired, as it were, a new home, for now the patriarchal traditions combined with others that had already taken root in certain places. Thus Jacob came to Bethel, where, as the account ran, it was once revealed to a human being in a dream by night that the 'gate of heaven' was there through which the messengers from the heavenly world came down to earth and went up again. But now, for the Israelites who settled round about Bethel, the recipient of that revelation was none other than Jacob himself. They claimed that particular tradition for their father Jacob, and at the same time they thereby claimed the sanctuary of Bethel for their God, the God of their father Jacob.

Just the same kind of thing happend to Abraham at the 'oaks of Mamre', the sanctuary near the town of Hebron. Here there was a story (we find it in Genesis 18) of a visit from three mysterious figures, who announced to the hospitable master of the household the future birth of a long-desired son and heir. For the immigrant Israelites the one to whom that meeting and promise had been granted could have been none other than their father Abraham. And behind the three figures there was hidden, in a way which in the last analysis remained inscrutable, the God of Abraham.

But at this point the picture of Abraham took on new features. For he had believed the promise, although from a human aspect everything spoke against it. His wife Sarah had no children, and was now past the age of child-bearing. But Abraham trusted the divine promise, and it was fulfilled for him. That picture of the believing and trusting Abraham now runs through the whole sequence of the narratives relating to him. Thus, in the impressive scene at night, when he looks at the starry sky and receives the promise that his descendants shall be as numerous as the stars, we are told quite simply that he 'believed in the Lord' – or, as it might be more aptly translated, he 'trusted'. But the text then goes on to say, according to the usual translation, that God 'reckoned it to him as righteousness' (Gen. 15.6). Here, too, it would be better to translate differently, as the word 'righteousness' suggests to us something quite different from the Hebrew word in the original text. The great Jewish philosopher and theologian Martin Buber, in his translation of the Bible, chose the word *Bewährung* – being put to the proof. Abraham 'stood the test' before God by trusting the promise against appearances.

Lastly, the picture of Abraham has been made particularly impressive by the passage that stands at the beginning of the narratives about him: 'Now the Lord said to Abram, "Go from your country, and your kindred, and your father's house to the land that I will show you"' (Gen. 12.1). Abraham obeys the command. Two things are indicated here: first, that the history of Israel begins with Abraham, with whom God began something quite new; and secondly, that that beginning was made in unconditional trust in God's promise and guidance.

With all this, the Israelite narrators did not turn Abraham into a saint. They repeatedly told how he doubted, and how, when the divine promises did not materialize, he tried to help them along with his own expedients. But that very fact shows us clearly how those traditions about Abraham were understood in Israel: they were the beginning of the nation's own history, and at the same time they showed the distinctive features of that history as it was experienced again by each generation. It was a history of divine promises and undertakings; but each generation faced anew the task of making those promises its own; and each generation in its turn was able to undergo the experience that, against human expectation and in spite of all doubt, the course of history was as God planned it.

Thus Abraham, the progenitor of one of the nomadic groups of the early period of Israel, had become the father of all Israel. His figure had acquired characteristics that went far beyond the bounds of the individual history of one person. He had become a prototype in whom Israel saw itself and its own history in outline, and in whom it could repeatedly recognize itself.

This emphasizes the importance of another sentence that occurs in the introductory words at the beginning of the story of Abraham. We read there: 'By you all the families of the earth shall be blessed' (Gen. 12.3). What Israel experienced and found prefigured in Abraham – the guidance of God, who repeatedly showed himself to be the Lord of history – concerned not only Israel, but the whole human race. If we speak of Israel's being 'elected' in the figure of Abraham, that means at the same time that it is entrusted with a service to all mankind: it means election, not for selfish purposes, but for a task in relation to the world as a whole. So Abraham becomes the father of all mankind, and that is what he has since increasingly become in proportion as the God of Israel has become the God of all nations.

In fixing the dates of the Mosaic period, especially for the stay in Egypt, we have extra-biblical sources for comparison. We are told in Ex. 1.11 that the Israelites were employed in the building of Pithom and Rameses. That points to the time of Pharaoh Rameses II, who had those two provisioning towns in the eastern delta of the Nile rebuilt. From Egyptian texts of the period, we learn that in times of drought nomadic groups were not infrequently allowed into Egyptian territory so as to be kept from starving. We are also told that foreign sections of the population were conscripted for forced labour.

Rameses II belonged to the dynasty of the Ramessids, and reigned from 1290 to 1224 BC. That is probably the time of the Israelites' exodus from Egypt.

Moses

The traditions that have come from the time of the patriarchs have one characteristic feature: the whole history takes the form of a family history. The people involved are man and wife, parents and children, and those in immediate contact with them; and the scene of the action is the family tent or somewhere not very far from it.

If we read on in the Old Testament, the picture suddenly changes. In the traditions that are collected in the Book of Exodus, Jacob's twelve sons and their families have become a nation. The history is now not of a family, but of a nation in its changing relationships with other nations; and the *dramatis personae* appear as representatives of their nations.

Again it is a towering figure who dominates the scene, and on whom, one might say, all the threads converge – Moses. His life's work is on a massive scale, and we meet him in the most varied situations. At the edge of the desert he is alone with his flock and his encounters with God; in the land of Egypt he represents his people before Pharaoh's throne, and leads them out of bondage into freedom; at the Red Sea the people under his leadership are saved from the Egyptians; on Mount Sinai it is he who talks with God on the people's behalf and receives the divine commandments; in the desert he guides the people through a series of new dangers and distresses; and when they are in sight of the promised land he gives them their last instructions before he dies.

Again the question arises, as with the patriarchs, 'Who was this Moses?' What kind of person was it of whom later generations could recount such great things, and whom they gave so distinguished a place in their nation's history? The student who approaches the texts with the methods of historical scrutiny must necessarily hesitate to regard this colossal picture of Moses simply as a biographical account of the life of one man. For it is a well-known phenomenon in the traditions about the beginnings of the history of many nations, that a later viewpoint brings events closer together, that incidents, originally unconnected, are joined one with another, and that tradition concentrates more and more on a few central figures.

Who was Moses? It is no longer possible for us to get a clear-cut picture of him; it is no use trying to write his biography. But in reading the texts, we can still feel something, not only of the impact that he must have made on his contemporaries, of the personal magnetism that emanated from him, and of the admiration with which he was regarded, but also of the resistance to him, and even of the deep-seated fear of him. He is shown as a great but at the same time an uncanny figure who cannot be contained within the framework of our own imagination.

Even his birth and childhood bear the stamp of the exceptional. He is exposed among the reeds of the Nile, to escape the Egyptians' murderous order that all newly born male babies were to be killed; he does not perish, but is taken to Pharaoh's court, where he grows up in safety. This account can hardly be a piece of authentic biography, for the ancient East can tell similar stories about other great figures. Of one of the first kings of the Land of the Two Rivers, Sargon of Akkad, the tradition runs that he was abandoned in the river soon after birth and was found there. The exceptional life of a great man demands an exceptional beginning.

The basic event, however, is Moses' meeting with God in the desert. As a fugitive in the country of the Midianites he is leading his father-in-law's flock along the edge of the desert, when suddenly he sees a strange and uncanny phenomenon – a blazing bush that is not being consumed. In ancient times anyone who hears of such a confrontation knows at once what is happening: a god has a communication to make to a human being. Moses, too, realizes this at once, and makes ready for the meeting with the god. The God who meets him there announces himself as the God of his fathers, Abraham, Isaac, and Jacob. But the word that now comes to Moses goes beyond what the fathers had learnt: this God tells him his name. At first, indeed, it is almost a veiling of the name: 'I am who I am', or, translated differently, 'I shall be who I shall be', or perhaps better still, 'I shall be there as the one who will be there' (Ex. 3.14). But in the Hebrew this 'I am' suggests 'Yahweh' ('Jehovah'), and finally this name, too, is uttered. It was Moses who first heard it.

It was he, too, who later led his people to Mount Sinai. Here, especially, the accounts stress the superhuman features in the picture of Moses. Even at a distance the effects of God's appearing in majesty on Mount Sinai would be more than the people could bear, but Moses goes up the mountain and stays there alone in the immediate neighbourhood of this God. We are even told (Num. 12.8) that God spoke with him 'mouth to mouth' as with one whom he trusted intimately. And he gives into his charge the instructions according to which the nation is to live as God's people.

We can see reflected here recollections of Israel's early experiences of God. Israel met this God in the wild grandeur of the landscape in the Sinai Peninsula. He has quite different characteristics from the God of the fathers; he is more severe and more demanding. And so Moses, too, is a figure of an entirely different type from the fathers. He faces the encounter, and he faces the people, who obey the divine command only with hesitation and anxiety, and then once more with grumbles and protests. In Moses the features of the later great prophetic figures are already anticipated.

But Moses is not shown to us merely as a prophet; he is also the political and military leader of his people. We see him standing up to Pharaoh and fighting for his people's freedom. We see him encouraging his fleeing people in sight of the pursuing Egyptians, and we see the people respect him after the wonderful deliverance. And again and again we see him as the man who leads the people on, through all the many dangers of the journey through the wilderness, and in spite of difficulties and hostility, to the end that God has preordained. So Moses becomes his people's deliverer, and thus the forerunner of later deliverers.

This part of the traditions, too, is based on memories of experiences that the Israelites had had. The story of Joseph and his brothers tells how the Israelites went to Egypt; in a long period of aridity and drought they had to go there if they were to keep themselves and their flocks alive. That was nothing unusual for the fertile country of Egypt, and Egyptian sources tell us the same kind of thing about other nomadic groups. Of course, the tradition has changed on one point, as it makes these events concern the whole of the Israelite people, and so anticipates something that did not take shape till later. The things that happened in Egypt and on Sinai were the experiences of particular groups that later became parts of the people of Israel. In retrospect, however, the whole of Israel saw in those experiences the basic events of its earlier history, and so they were extended to become experiences of the whole people; and Moses, who was the leader of one of those groups, became the pioneer and leader of all Israel. As in the case of the traditions of the fathers, we have here an extension and a generalizing of early Israelite history. For later generations Israel was so very much a unity, and the consciousness of that unity was so formative and decisive, that even its early history had to be fused into an undivided whole. And just as Abraham became the father of all Israel, so Moses became the leader and deliverer of the whole people.

But one feature in the picture of Moses has had the greatest after-effects of all: it is through him that the people of Israel were given the 'law'. The word 'torah', which we translate as 'law', really means 'direction(s)' or instruction(s)'. It is the direction for life – life before God and life within the human society; the commandments that are given to the people of Israel are to help them to live. Speaking generally, the word 'law' suggests something quite different to us; it suggests a hard, relentless, soulless demand, and when we hear it in its theological sense against the background of New Testament texts, it sounds just like self-redemption of the man who will not trust divine grace. Any such understanding of the law is entirely foreign to the Old Testament, especially in its early days.

The directions and commandments that are associated with

the name of Moses cover the most diverse spheres of life. In the decalogue, the ten commandments, it is a matter of elementary rules of corporate human life: 'You shall not kill. You shall not commit adultery. You shall not steal.' These are not severe demands, cramping a person's life; they are necessary and beneficent ordinances that begin to make it possible for people to live together. No society can endure without such ordinances, and Israel formulated them at the outset of its history, and saw them direct its life in the family, among kith and kin, and in the nation at large. And in this respect it cared particularly for the poor and defenceless, for widows and orphans. We find the instruction that a blind man is not to be misled on his way; and even the animals are thought of when it is laid down that anyone who sees another person's (even his enemy's) ass that has collapsed under its burden, is to help it up again. The directions given here are thoroughly humanitarian.

But there are other commandments, too. Many of them, dealing with matters concerning worship, we now feel to be far removed from us – regulations about sacrifices and purity, and many details of religious formalities. But here, too, we are dealing, not with the soulless demands of a rigid formal observance, but with further applications of the one maxim 'I am the Lord your God', which is carried further in another passage to 'You shall be holy, for I the Lord your God am holy.' No religion can do without such rules. Of course, they are more subject to changes of outlook and insight, so that they have moved further from us. But Israel needed them in order to live.

Later tradition has attached this multiplicity of directions, commandments, and laws to the name of Moses. Here we see once again the same kind of summarizing as in the earlier traditions, their concentration on particular figures. As in a prism, the many rays of Israel's varied legislation through the centuries converge on Moses. He stands at the beginning of the whole series, and so his authority was claimed for all the later periods as well. For it was through him that Israel was given the essential foundations of its life.

But not only Israel lives on these ordinances. The first Christians took their validity for granted; and even though it may seem at first sight that Paul, in opposing a certain attitude that was being taken in his own time about the law, wanted to annul everything that went with Moses, the basic ordinances themselves remained in force without question. The ten commandments became almost a Magna Carta for the human race, and the rules of corporate life in our world of today are profoundly influenced by the directions that were set out for it at the beginning of Israel's history. So Moses, like Abraham, outgrows the narrow confines of the people of Israel and becomes one of the fathers of mankind.

The figure of Joshua is closely associated with the period when the Israelites settled in the land of Canaan and 'possessed the land'. The exact time of the occupation cannot be determined, especially as it was probably a gradual process which may have extended over several generations. Some indication of dates may be had from the exodus from Egypt during the reign of Rameses II (see p. 18). Besides this, his successor Merneptah mentions in an inscription on his famous 'stele', a victory over 'Israel' in the land of Canaan about 1220 BC, though in fact it is uncertain just what 'Israel' means here. Lastly, we must suppose that the occupation was completed some considerable time before the establishment of the Israelite monarchy, which took place round about 1000 BC. It thus seems that the occupation may have taken place in the thirteenth or twelfth century BC.

Joshua

The great figures of Israel's earlier history, Abraham and Moses, belong to a time when the Israelite tribes had not yet settled in the country that was later to become their homeland, but were still living with their flocks and tents in the steppe country on the edge of the cultivated land. It was a crucial turning-point in their way of living when they made this country, in which they had so far only temporarily pastured their flocks, their permanent place of residence, when they exchanged the untrammelled life of the tent-dweller for a settled residence in fixed places, and made farming and vine-growing, instead of cattle-raising, the basis of their economic life.

At this crucial turning-point there stands in the tradition the figure of Joshua; it was he who led the tribes across the Jordan; under his leadership they conquered the country; and finally, it was he who allotted land to the individual tribes, and so determined the future territory of each. As in the case of the patriarchs and Moses, we have to assume that in the picture that the texts give of him a great deal has coalesced, that events have been gathered together retrospectively and in a certain sense generalized. For the people of Israel felt that the period of the occupation, too, formed an essential part of their common early history; and so in their tradition it was increasingly depicted from a unified viewpoint.

In those events Joshua had a decisive part to play; he formed the bridge between the period before the occupation, when the people lived in the desert under Moses' guidance, and the new period, which began when they settled. The Old Testament texts persistently reflect the consciousness that they are dealing here with two quite distinct and clearly separated stages in the history of the people of Israel. That consciousness is emphasized by the persistent assertion that the entire generation that had experienced the great events in Egypt and at Sinai was not allowed to enter the promised land. In particular, Moses himself was not allowed to enter the land into which he was to lead the Israelites. He was allowed only to see it from a distance, from Mount Nebo, before he died. It was reserved for Joshua to complete his work.

The authors of the Old Testament texts were repeatedly concerned with the peculiar tension between this promise and its fulfilment. They found its explanation in the Israelites' lack of trust in the divine guidance during the wandering in the desert, in their disobedience towards Moses who was divinely commissioned to lead them. This theme of the people's disobedience and 'murmuring' comes out in numerous narratives. Only two men of that generation, Caleb and Joshua, were finally allowed to enter the promised land; even Moses himself had to suffer with the people as their representative, and die before the Jordan was crossed. The leadership was now in the hands of Joshua.

According to the tradition, he was a man who had been made fit for his task in a special way. He is shown as Moses' constant companion and most intimate confidant. On Sinai he is the only one by Moses' side, in close proximity to God, while the people are making a god for themselves in the golden calf. He serves in the holy tent and guards it during Moses' absence. And on Moses' instructions he wages war against the Amalekites, Israel's hereditary enemy. Lastly, he is formally commissioned as Moses' successor, and we are told that he was 'full of the spirit of wisdom', because Moses had transferred his office to him by laying his hands on him. At the same time the gap between the two men is emphasized when it is said that there had 'not arisen a prophet since in Israel like Moses' (Deut. 34.10). Joshua continues the work, but he is no second Moses. He is responsible for a definite task, but he is not in the line of the great figures of Israel's early period.

Joshua's main work begins when the Israelites cross the Jordan. If we look at the picture of him given by the two parts of the tradition before and after that crucial event, we see that in the first of them his characteristics are remarkably vague. He is Moses' companion, but he is hardly ever shown as acting on his own account. In the second part, however, the lines of the picture are more distinct. We must probably assume that historically speaking, his proper place is to be found in the period after the occupation, and that it was only in the condensing and unifying of the traditions that his figure was pushed across into the time of the desert wanderings – as a connecting link between the two periods.

In the Book of Joshua the accounts of the crossing of the Jordan, and of the period directly following, show Joshua as the people's leader in a very varied light. The actual crossing of the Jordan is described as a solemn ceremony. On the divine command, the priests march with the ark of the covenant across the Jordan, which divides as did once the waters of the Red Sea before the Israelites led by Moses. All the people follow in a body. Perhaps this account reflects the presentation of a religious act performed regularly to celebrate the crossing of the Jordan. In any case, it is certain that the events were later stylized so as to give posterity a suitable expression of their significance. In this connection Joshua appears almost as a priest.

Again, the narrative of the capture of Jericho almost suggests the description of a religious ceremony. The Israelites march in solemn procession round the city for seven days, till at the final march, when the rams' horns are sounded and the people suddenly raise their war-cry, the city walls collapse. But here a new feature is added: the miraculous nature of the event. The text obviously seeks to bring this point out specially, that it is not the Israelites' military strength, but a divine miracle, that has brought the city down. Joshua appears again here as the one who carries out the divine commands and thereby prepares the way for the miracle.

This same text makes it quite clear how in the person of Joshua a definite picture of this period of Israel's history took shape. The land that God promised them did not fall to them through their own strength, but was given to them by God in a miraculous way; and Joshua was the instrument that he used for his miracles.

But who, in fact, was Joshua? How are these narratives related to the actual historical events? This question has been the subject of very lively discussion among scholars, especially in recent times. It has been raised again by the fact that archaeology has thrown new light on the historical facts of the period. Jericho, and other places mentioned in the biblical tradition, have been excavated from the rubble of many centuries, and the advance of archaeological methods has made it possible for us to determine with more and more certainty the age of the various layers that have been uncovered. It has thus been shown that the city's great walls were not destroyed for the first time by the immigrant Israelites, but that they must have already fallen several centuries earlier through military action or natural catastrophe.

What can we make of this for our understanding of these narratives and for our judgment of the figure of Joshua? It would certainly be wrong to say that the narratives were simply 'invented'. Rather we must try to enter, in imagination, into the origin of such ancient traditions. The consciousness that the country in which the Israelites were living had been given to them by God was expressed in many ways, and in particular it crystallized into fairly detailed narratives centring on specially impressive incidents. Such an incident was the finding of the mighty walls of Jericho lying in ruins. What was more obvious than to connect their destruction with the events of the occupation of the country? The walls of Jericho became, as it were, a symbol of the whole of that significant period, and the figure of Joshua became the point on which all the current traditions relating to the period centred – as had been the case with Abraham and Moses in their own times.

But beside these there are texts in which Joshua appears in a very different light. As the Israelites' military leader he defeats the Canaanites' troops and conquers their cities. In some cases these accounts have been confirmed by archaeological discoveries. That is true, for instance, of the great city of Hazor, in the northern part of the country; its capture is reported in Joshua 11, and it has quite recently been excavated by archaeologists. It actually was destroyed by military action at the time of the Israelite occupation. Thus the picture that the texts give of Joshua is by no means a mere product of later imagination; it has a clearly recognizable historical basis, round which further traditional features have accumulated in the course of time.

According to the accounts in the second part of the Book of Joshua, it also fell to Joshua to divide the land among the different tribes. As, however, the occupation took a considerable time to complete, events here are again packed more closely together. But there are important and interesting indications that Joshua's authority actually was recognized by all the tribes. It is reported in Joshua 17, for instance, that when the 'house of Joseph', which means the tribes of Ephraim and Manasseh, came to him with the complaint that their territory was too small, he allotted them certain as yet uncolonized forest districts to clear and inhabit. Here Joshua appears as a court of appeal to whom the tribes could bring their wishes and grievances, and whose verdict was then recognized by everyone. The same kind of thing is reported later about Samuel, so that in this matter we may regard Joshua as a forerunner of the 'judges' of the later period. And in that capacity he certainly influenced the final distribution and demarcation of the territories occupied by the different tribes, as reported by the tradition.

There is another passage that shows Joshua's importance for the tribes of Israel as a whole. It is reported in Joshua 24 that he gathered all Israel to Shechem, and that he there pledged the people formally to make a solemn covenant to worship only Yahweh, the God of Israel. Here Joshua is the one who played a decisive part in making Israel a religious community worshipping one God. It is expressly stated that the fathers, when they were still 'beyond the River' (the Euphrates), served other gods, and this possibility is also taken into account in the existing situation after the occupation; so the Israelites are required to abandon other gods and to serve this God alone. For Israel can be Israel only by serving this one God. This passage shows clearly that in religion too Israel became a unified community only by degrees, and in this connection again the figure of Joshua is of fundamental importance.

Thus the crucial period of transition, when Israel established its new existence as one community on the soil of the promised land, is summed up in Joshua. In the account of the ending of his life's work, in Joshua 23, we are told that not one of the promises that God had made to the people had failed, but that everything had been fulfilled and had come to pass. The fulfilment of the promises, which had been delayed in such a peculiar way by the death of Moses and his generation, had now finally come about through Joshua.

The period following the Israelites' occupation is marked by changes in the balance of power in the area where they had settled. Up to about 1200 BC it was dominated by the Egyptians, who lost it about that time through the invasion of a great surge of migrants from the eastern Mediterranean regions, the so-called People of the Sea. One section of these, the Philistines, settled on the coastal plains. They tried to take over the country as its overlords in succession to the Egyptians, and in doing so they clashed with the Israelites, who on their side claimed to rule the region where they had settled. Besides this, the Israelites had to defend their territory on the east against the Ammonites, Moabites, and Edomites, who had settled about the same time east of the Jordan, as well as against what was left of the Canaanite forces. This eventful struggle was not decided in favour of the Israelites till the time of David.

Samuel

The changed pattern of living from nomadic existence to permanent settlement on cultivated land also meant a new pattern of community life. At first the Israelites kept their tribal organizations. But they were conscious of belonging to something larger than their own particular tribe, and they united to form larger or smaller tribal federations. Here, no doubt, an important part was played by their differentiation from the previous inhabitants of the country, the Canaanites. At first, indeed, it would be a comparatively loose organization that joined the tribes together; we see this very clearly in contrast to the other peoples of the country. With these the normal form of government was always a monarchy, whether in the form of small city kingdoms as in the case of the Canaanites and Philistines, or as a national kingdom as in the case of the eastern and southern neighbours, the Ammonites, Moabites, and Edomites.

In the early days after the occupation Israel had no monarchy, and we do not know what kind of legal and governmental organization the federated tribes had among themselves. Religious elements, too, presumably gave them some feeling of unity, especially the common worship of Yahweh at certain sanctuaries. And in the setting of that more or less close union there now repeatedly emerge the names of outstanding leaders whom we usually call 'judges'. On the one hand, they appeared in times of distress as military leaders of the Israelite tribes; in such cases we often read that the Spirit of God came upon them and qualified them to be leaders, as happened to Gideon; but on the other hand, we are also told that they 'judged' Israel – a statement probably implying that they took a leading part in the administration of justice.

The last of the great figures before the inauguration of the monarchy is Samuel. We find united in him all the features that characterized the different aspects of the office of 'judge', while at the same time the picture that we have of him also contains quite different elements, which make him stand out far above the 'judges' and give him a unique place in the history of Israel. In particular, tradition makes him play a decisive part in establishing an Israelite monarchy.

As in the case of Moses, we have been given a story of the miraculous circumstances of his birth. In the first chapters of I Samuel we are told that his mother Hannah had been childless for many years. At last, while she was praying in the temple at Shiloh for a son, she made a vow that she would dedicate him to service at the sanctuary. She gave birth to a son, and Samuel came to the sanctuary at Shiloh. As with Moses, we can hardly take this story of his birth as a strictly biographical account. It contains a number of typical motifs such as we meet both in the Old Testament and elsewhere. Thus the motif of childlessness occurs with Sarah the mother of Isaac, with Rebekah the mother of Jacob, with Rachel the mother of Joseph and Benjamin, and with Samson's mother, whose name is not given. In some of the narratives a part is played by rivalry and jealousy between a man's two wives, as, for instance, between Rachel and Leah; and this also occurs in the story of Samuel's birth. There is one more thing to be noticed: In the Hebrew narrative there is a play on the name Samuel. We are told that Hannah named her son 'Samuel', 'for she said, "I have asked him of the Lord"' (I Sam. 1.20). But the Hebrew word 'to (obtain by) request' has actually less resemblance to the name Samuel (Hebrew *shemu'el*) than to the name Saul (*shā'ûl*), which means 'the one asked for' or 'obtained by asking'. Is it possible here that a story about the birth of Saul, the first king of Israel, was transferred to his great antagonist Samuel?

However that may be, the story will in any case explain Samuel's close connection with the temple in Shiloh, and it points to certain priestly features in his picture. But then, at the end of the part dealing with his youth, the account says: 'And all Israel from Dan to Beersheba knew that Samuel was established as a prophet of the Lord' (I Sam. 3.20). To the picture of the priest there is here added that of the prophet. The tradition asserts repeatedly that Samuel stood in an exceptionally close relationship to God, as was characteristic of the prophets of later times. Even in the story of his youthful days in the temple God speaks to him at night, and when he at last realizes who is speaking to him, he replies: 'Speak, for thy servant hears.' Here, for the first time, he is directly addressed by God. Later we are told repeatedly that he received definite instructions from God, with whom he had direct conversation; and we see him, too, interceding for his people in a distressing situation. We also see here how strikingly the picture of him resembles that of Moses. The explanation of this similarity may be that some later prophetic circles considered Moses and Samuel to be their immediate forerunners, and therefore set out to elaborate these particular features in the tradition.

But Samuel is not only a priest and prophet; he is also a 'judge'. This side of his work is emphasized several times, and we are given interesting details of it. Thus we are told that he went round year by year fulfilling his judicial office at various places – places that played an important part in Israel's history, and were in some cases well-known sanctuaries: Bethel, Gilgal, Mizpah, and Ramah where Samuel himself lived. Obviously, therefore, his judicial functions were of special importance for Israel. It might well seem as if the features that are united in this one person were too varied – on the one hand priest and prophet, directly involved in the sphere of religion and ceremonies, and on the other hand the judge, responsible for the matter-of-fact and quite non-religious business of administering justice. But that would be to adopt a modern point of view, and, in particular, to regard law and justice in a way that does not correspond to the ideas of ancient times. Not only in Israel, but also elsewhere in the ancient East, law was directly related to the sphere of the divine, and the administration of justice was often closely associated with religion. In Israel's early history there certainly seems to have been a definite way of establishing the legal rights of a case, with help, in difficult cases, from a person who was regarded as specially enlightened by God, and so, as it were, directly commissioned by God to give the verdict. In the picture of Moses we already find this combination of prophetic and judicial features; and in the Book of Judges we are told that 'Deborah, a prophetess . . . was judging Israel at that time' (Judg. 4.4). So we can see Samuel in that line of 'prophetic judges'.

But Samuel's special place in Israel's history is mainly due to the fact that he stood on the threshold between two epochs; for with him the period of the judges ended, and after him that of the kings began. That transition, however, was made not without friction, but under stresses and difficulties; and, according to tradition, it was Samuel who had to bear the brunt of the altercations. It is certainly not easy to be sure what part he actually played in all this, for the biblical accounts contain striking contradictions. It is agreed that he instituted Saul as the first King of Israel; but the proceedings themselves and their background are the subject of two entirely different narratives, which contradict each other on certain crucial points.

One of the accounts, in I Samuel 9-10, tells us, in a popular style, how Saul, a young man from the tribe of Benjamin, set out to look for his father's asses which had strayed, and how on the way he met the prophet Samuel quite by chance, and by divine command was secretly anointed by him to be king over Israel. So here the initiative in setting up a king is taken by Samuel himself on divine instructions.

In the other account, the matter is presented in an entirely different way: the people's elders meet and demand of Samuel the appointment of a king, saying expressly that they want to have a king, 'like all the nations'. Samuel sees in this an attack on his office; but in prayer he receives the divine answer that the people's demand is directed, not against him, but against God; 'for they have not rejected you, but they have rejected me from being king over them' (I Sam. 8.7). That is a caustic and fundamental repudiation of monarchy in general as an institution. That its establishment is, after all, finally allowed appears to be a concession to the people's lack of discernment; but it will, in the nature of things, lead to its own ruin.

How is this contradiction to be explained? It is obvious that there were in Israel differing opinions about royalty, at different times and in different circles. There seem to have been circles that rejected it outright. The question of such an office had already arisen once: in the story of Gideon, one of those 'judges' who as military leader delivered the people out of a desperate plight, we read that, after defeating the enemy, the Israelites offered him the dignity of kingship, which he refused with the words: 'I will not rule over you, and my son will not rule over you; the Lord will rule over you' (Judg. 8.23). So here, too, the contrast is formulated between a human kingship over Israel and a divine kingship. There were in Israel circles that regarded their people as God's people in such a literal sense that they saw in the establishment of a monarchy a defection from God. But there was evidently another view of things, and this was based, above all, on the threat to Israel from its hostile neighbours the Philistines. Military strength sufficient to counter this threat needed a strict unified leadership, such as no one but a king could ensure in the existing circumstances. So for many people a king was a historical necessity.

The historian's hindsight will take into account another aspect: in the decades or centuries since they had settled, the Israelite tribes had grown closer and closer together, and had become increasingly one people instead of being merely a number of tribes more or less loosely united. And a logical consequence of this development was that the people created for themselves an appropriate system of living as one community. But for that particular period such a system had to be a monarchy after the pattern of the neighbouring peoples.

So this step that Israel took into a new epoch of its history could hardly have been avoided. But it brought with it its own problems, as is the case, in greater or less degree, with every kind of human society. For such a system can never do justice to all requirements and all wishes on an equal basis. And above all, when religious traditions clash with the requirements of state policy, there are bound to be tensions and oppositions. In the course of their history the people of Israel have never quite settled those problems. And later generations saw in retrospect that Samuel had stood at a turning-point in the nation's history, and that he was the first to experience and sustain the whole weight of those problems. So, while it is true that Samuel belongs to the great men of Israel's history, he remains fundamentally a tragic figure.

Towards the end of the second millennium BC, northwards of the land settled by the Israelites, other peoples had also established themselves – the Arameans. They, too, had gone over from a nomadic to a settled way of life; they had established themselves in many districts of Mesopotamia and Syria, and so formed a whole series of new independent states. When David began to extend his authority, it meant a conflict with the Arameans living to the east and southeast of the Anti-Lebanon, especially with the state of Damascus, which played a leading part. David succeeded in gaining the mastery over them for the duration of his own reign, and also over his southwestern neighbours the Philistines, as well as those to the east and south-east, the Ammonites, Moabites, and Edomites (cf. II Sam. 8).

We know the approximate dates of David's reign. The earliest date of which we can be quite certain in the history of Israel is the year of Solomon's death, 926. The biblical tradition has it, in round figures, that each reigned forty years. From this we may infer that David's reign began round about 1000 BC.

David

The new form of government, the monarchy that began with Saul, did not have happy omens. It evidently met with opposition on religious grounds from the outset, and a conflict between Samuel and the king whom he had set up seems soon to have come to a head. The tradition tells, in one way or another, of Saul's disobedience to certain cultic demands, and of serious dissensions between the two men. And at last the account says that an 'evil spirit' came upon Saul and tormented him. That evil spirit, however, is simply the counterpart of the Spirit of God, which we are previously told had come upon him. Saul was still quite in line with the 'judges' who had preceded him, in that at first, long before he was called on to be king, he had been enabled by the divine Spirit to take over the leadership of the Israelite tribes and deliver them from their enemies. But then, we are told, that Spirit left him and gave place to an evil spirit. So the tradition makes clear the existence of a peculiar state of affairs: Saul is still king, but he is already rejected: and the other man, who is to be king in his place, is already secretly chosen. His name is David.

The story of David's rise to kingship shows striking parallels to that of Saul. In each case a homely shepherd boy is suddenly brought out into the bright light of history. In each case Samuel is commanded by God to anoint the new king in secret, avoiding publicity. And lastly we are told of David, as we were previously told of Saul, that the Spirit of God came upon him.

The unusually keen interest of subsequent narrators in the events leading up to this outstanding monarchy can also be seen in the existence of the two different accounts of how David came to the court of King Saul. One of these, in I Samuel 16, says that a man was sought who would look after the king, and in particular free him, through music, from the torment of the evil spirit, and that the choice fell on David. But the other account, in the following chapter, runs quite differently: in the war against the Philistines the Israelites were terrified by the Philistines' champion fighter, a giant named Goliath, who challenged the Israelite army and demanded an opponent for a duel. David, the shepherd boy, happened to be there on one occasion when Goliath was challenging and mocking the Israelites; he stripped for action and killed the heavily armed Philistine with nothing more than a stone from a sling such as shepherds used for scaring off beasts of prey.

Both of these accounts already contain the germ of rivalry between David and Saul, which results in David's fleeing from him and being pursued by him for a long time. Here again there is particular emphasis on how low Saul has sunk. He pursues his former armour-bearer and successful army commander, because he sees his kingship threatened by him; and at last, in a battle against the Philistines, he dies ingloriously by his own hand.

This episode brings to an end the unhappy first phase of the monarchy in Israel. And now there begins a new period that brings Israel to an undreamt-of national greatness, and makes it for some decades the predominant power in the whole area of Syria and Palestine. This great epoch in Israel's history is indissolubly linked with the name of David. We are certainly not exaggerating if we describe David as a political and military genius. First of all, he succeeded in uniting the Israelite tribes for the first time under a single firm leadership. We do not know exactly how far the area of Saul's rule actually extended; but we see that after his death a breach opened between the northern and the southern tribes, and David had first to close this. He ended by uniting two kingships in his own person – one over Judah in the south, and the other over the remaining tribes in the north and east.

The next step shows very clearly his wise and far-sighted policy. The question where he would set up his residence was bound to arise. Should he choose one of the cities that already had the status of a capital in one part of his territory? But would not the other part then regard this as a discrimination against it? David took a different course. Just on the border between the two areas now united under him, there was a small and unimportant Canaanite town. Perhaps the only reason why it was not yet in Israelite hands was that there was no point in making any particular effort to capture it. It did not lie on any of the more important trade routes either, so it had simply been bypassed. It was called Jerusalem. David marched with his personal band of mercenaries, his bodyguard, captured the town, and made it his personal independent residence, thus adding to his twofold kingship a third – that of the city of Jerusalem.

But David was not content merely to create an independent residence; he increased the prestige of his capital by taking another important step; he brought the ark of the covenant, the sacred religious symbol of the Israelite tribes, to Jerusalem, and by this means made the city the centre of religious life. The great part played by Jerusalem in later centuries in the history of Israel and Judaism, as well as of Christianity and Islam, has its roots here.

Thus David had united the Israelites and given them a common centre. Now he could proceed to extend his rule further. The first and most dangerous opponents with whom he had to deal were the Philistines, against whom Saul had come to grief. Here, too, David proved his military skill; he defeated the Philistines, and so decided the question of supremacy in the land finally and unequivocally in favour of the Israelites. But that brought him further territories, for those still occupied by the Canaanites were at that time dominated by the Philistines. These, too, now formed part of the increasingly large area that he ruled. And the neighbours in the south and east, too, had to submit to him; he subdued the kingdoms of the Ammonites, Moabites, and Edomites, and incorporated them in his own. And finally, he even succeeded in pushing forward a long way to the north and subjugating the extensive Aramean states whose centre was Damascus, so that his authority reached as far as the Euphrates. He thus created a larger realm than has existed, before or since, in those territories, and politically he took Israel to a height that it has never again reached.

In this, however, he was favoured by the circumstances of his time. Foreign great powers had repeatedly, for many centuries, interested themselves in that narrow strip of cultivated land formed by Syria and Palestine at the eastern end of the Mediterranean; and for a long time the Egyptians in the south and the Hittites in the north had fought for predominance there. But their power had passed; and the great powers of the Land of the Two Rivers, the Assyrians and Babylonians, and later the Persians, had not yet appeared on the stage of history to assert their claims to the territory. In the few centuries during which the country was allowed to pause for breath, David was able to establish his sway over a large area – the only time that this has been done there by the native peoples.

So it is not surprising that David has taken an outstanding place in the consciousness of later generations. For posterity he was simply the King, for the dynasty that bore his name ruled in Jerusalem for more than four hundred years. But it was not only in the political and military spheres that he was regarded as a model. In later historical narratives the kings were also judged by their attitude to religion; and no verdict on a king could be more positive than this, that 'he walked in all the way of David his father', for David was the king after God's heart. And we are told more than once that for David's sake his descendants should not bear the full burden of their iniquities; for it was said that God himself had promised David that there should always be one of his descendants on the throne.

Lastly, it is in this promise that there is rooted the expectation that there will eventually come from David's lineage a king with whom the day of salvation for the whole world will dawn, the expectation of the 'Messiah', as we say. The further the reality of the Israelite monarchy departed from the great ideal of its earliest days, and the more restricted Israel's political power was, the stronger the expectation grew that some day a new 'star out of Jacob' would rise, as the old text has it (Num. 24.17). This expectation was clearly expressed for the first time in the words of the prophet Isaiah. At a time of great distress caused by the Assyrians, the prophet predicts the coming of a king who will be a 'prince of peace', and of whose government there will be no end. What David once gave to his people, peace and stable government, this king of salvation will finally bring about in a way far surpassing David himself. In another passage from Isaiah the expectation is raised to an even higher pitch. The king of salvation, who will emerge like a new shoot from the old stem of the Davidic dynasty, will not only be the bearer of the Spirit of God, like David himself and, before him, the judges and Moses; and he will not only establish perfect righteousness among men; when he comes, all disturbing factors in the corporate life of human beings and animals on this earth will cease. Beasts of prey will lie down peacefully among other animals, little children will play with serpents which are now the worst enemies of human beings, and nothing that is evil or destructive will exist any more.

But it is characteristic of the messianic expectation expressed in the Old Testament that these 'paradisal' conditions are not the real core of the hope, but that one particular element is persistently stressed: the establishment of perfect righteousness among men. That is what is regarded, in the long run, as the root of the matter – as the crucial lack in the present realities of life, and as the crucial blessing that is to be finally expected from the king of salvation. If everyone is treated justly, then corporate life has attained the perfection that is its right object.

Thus the memory of David has been kept alive through the centuries by the messianic hope. His forceful personality left its mark so effectively that later generations have repeatedly gone back to him to get their bearings. But his descendants were not able to preserve his large area of rule. It was so very much his own work, and it so urgently needed a strong personality, such as David had been, that it survived him for only one generation.

The period of Solomon's rule was marked by active diplomatic relations with foreign states; but for all that, he could not hold David's realm together. Even during his lifetime the Arameans re-established their independence and formed a new kingdom in Damascus. The Edomites and Ammonites, too, regained their independence, either during his lifetime or directly afterwards. After Solomon's death in 926 BC, David's realm disintegrated completely.

Solomon

Through the empire created by David, Israel had become the predominant power in the whole of Syria and Palestine. For the course that history was now to take, it was of great importance who his successor was to be. II Samuel gives us a vivid picture of the disputes, both open and secret, that grew out of this question; they came to such a pitch that once David had to save himself by flight when his son Absalom had himself proclaimed king. Finally, David himself decided the question and handed his kingdom over to his son Solomon.

It is not merely from a historical point of view that the account of the disputes about the succession to David's throne is a most interesting document. We must regard it as a first-rate literary achievement, especially as it represents a type of literature that was quite new in ancient Israel; it is the first work that we can describe as historical writing in the true sense. What we meet in previous times is primarily traditions in the form of legend, which is not directly interested in the historical circumstances themselves, but presents them in a particular light as an occurrence of an illustrative and typical nature, suggesting the presence, at the time, of the narrator and his hearers. It was only gradually that there developed the ability, which is needed before there can be any really historical writing, to observe and present the facts out of the consciousness of historical distance. The tradition of the succession to David's throne is, in fact, the first example of a continuous historical narrative in Israel, and it shows how artistically this kind of literature was already being handled, even at such an early stage.

It is no accident that this new kind of historical writing appears at this particular time. For there was developing at the royal court an intellectual and cultural life that created entirely new conditions. The tradition records this characteristic when it speaks of Solomon's 'wisdom'. Something of what this wisdom implies can be seen in I Kings 4 and 5. We are told first that his wisdom 'surpassed the wisdom of all the peoples of the east, and all the wisdom of Egypt.' This means that international standards are applied, and we can already see here a basic feature of the new court life: it is in touch with other countries, and in particular it assimilates a good deal from the great ancient civilizations of the Euphrates and the Nile. But it seems that at the same time there developed in Israel during Solomon's reign a cultural life with a pattern of its own.

Thus we are also told of Solomon that 'he uttered three thousand proverbs; and his songs were a thousand and five'. As to the subject matter of those proverbs and songs, it is said that they dealt with natural objects: 'of trees, from the cedar that is in Lebanon to the hyssop that grows out of the wall', and with many kinds of large and small animals. From that description it is clear that behind Solomon's wisdom there is a definite kind of science such as we also know from the ancient East. In Egyptian literature especially there are enumerations, something like lists, of objects either of nature or from other fields of knowledge, evidently intended to collect and arrange the sum total of what is known, as a kind of encyclopaedia of knowledge. Such natural science in the form of a 'science of lists' was probably also cultivated in the Israelite court in Jerusalem. But what was distinctive about it here seems to have been that the objects were not merely enumerated, but that they were put into the form of proverbs and songs. In this way Solomon's wisdom was 'greater' than that of the other nations.

But this wisdom embraced more than the realm of nature. The so-called 'proverbs of Solomon', at least some of which probably do go back to the time of Solomon himself, contain quite different themes as well. Above all, there are many rules for human social life, and particularly for behaviour at court and towards people in higher positions; and this again shows quite clearly that the royal court was the place where this wisdom was cultivated. There had now developed here a cosmopolitan outlook that radically changed the intellectual situation in Israel.

We can also see this in the attitude towards certain religious traditions. If, for instance, we compare the historical work which we have already mentioned, dealing with the succession to David's throne, with the older narratives, we realize at once that the way in which God's action in historical events is spoken of has undergone a fundamental change. Thus in the narratives of the patriarchs and Moses we are repeatedly told that God himself spoke to men, and we read of direct and often miraculous intervention in the course of events. There is nothing of all this in the story of the succession to the throne; the occurrences are described from a purely human standpoint; their causal connection is traced without reference to God, and only occasionally is it directly indicated that God so disposed the matter. It is true that the author of this historical work is of the opinion that God directs events; but he sees him at work right behind the scenes, so that the *dramatis personae* often know nothing about it, and it is only in retrospect that they can say that God so ordained it. It is therefore a much freer – one might almost say a more enlightened – spirit that is at work here. And we are bound to say that this spirit has had for the entire later history of Israelite thought and faith an importance that can hardly be overestimated.

But there was another sphere in which Solomon exercised a lasting influence. David had made Jerusalem his residence; Solomon developed it into a capital. He erected a royal palace on a grand scale, and, directly connected with it, a temple. In I Kings we have a detailed account of the building, and this shows quite clearly that here, too, foreign models had a strong influence. The architects and workmen came from the Phoenician coastal towns with their much older and highly developed civilization; and the design of the palace and temple relied on models in other countries.

It was above all in the building of the temple that the importance of Jerusalem as the intellectual and religious centre of all

Israel was more firmly established. David had already begun to move in that direction by taking to Jerusalem the ark of the covenant, the ancient sacred symbol of the Israelite tribes. But during his reign it remained in a modest tent; now it was taken in solemn state to the temple, and set up there in the holy of holies. There could now develop here a form of worship in which all the varied traditions that the Israelite tribes had brought with them into the country, and everything that had developed since by way of cultic traditions and customs, came together. The picture of the Israelite religion, as it is presented to us in the Old Testament, is quite definitely determined by this concentration of religious and cultic traditions at this one point, the temple that Solomon built in Jerusalem. Mount Zion, on which the temple stood, was henceforth the place where Israel was conscious in a special way of the presence of its God, and where it came together to worship him.

Thus the importance of Solomon lay above all in the cultivation of intellectual and cultural life. His international relationships were reflected in a vigorous diplomatic activity, one aspect of which was that numerous daughters of foreign kings and princes lived in the large harem that he kept after the style of oriental monarchs. Besides this, he had active trading relationships with all parts of the then known world. He failed, however, to maintain the great empire that his father David had created, for he could not prevent various neighbouring peoples whom David had subjected from regaining their independence.

At home, too, difficulties loomed up, for there was a reverse side to Solomon's grandiose royal household. It was, of course, very expensive, and the expense had to be made good by the country over which he ruled. That undoubtedly imposed a great burden on the population of Israel, and the burden was increased by the fact that Solomon's extensive building programme, much of which has been brought to light by recent excavations, meant that the Israelites were subjected to forced labour. In that respect too, therefore, he ruled exactly in the style of an oriental despot, in contrast to the old Israelite tradition, which left no room for the assumption of such arbitrary power by one ruler. Lastly, he was prepared to make very far-reaching concessions in religious matters by setting up to the east of the city, in the area now known as the Mount of Olives, sanctuaries for foreign deities, so as to enable his foreign wives and their attendants to practise their native forms of worship.

So an internal crisis was almost bound to come. The tradition tells us (in I Kings 11) that a man named Jeroboam, whom Solomon had put in charge of the forced labour in Jerusalem because of his efficiency, ventured on a revolt against the king. And it is no accident that a prophet, Ahijah of Shiloh, had a hand in this; for the new kingdom's abuses roused indignation on behalf of the genuine Israelite tradition.

The revolt failed, and Jeroboam fled to Egypt. But he was to reappear a little later on the stage of history; for it became apparent that only Solomon in person had been able to hold together any longer the empire that David had created. When Solomon died, about the year 926 BC, the crisis was at once plain to all. It is true that his son Rehoboam tried, like David and Solomon, to unite in his own person the monarchy over all the Israelite tribes. But after dramatic negotiations, in which he refused to give up the kind of domination that his father had developed, the northern tribes and those east of the Jordan seceded and set up their own kingdom, giving their allegiance to Jeroboam. Only the tribe of Judah in the south, and apparently the small tribe of Benjamin, were left to be ruled by Rehoboam and so by the dynasty that David had founded. That was the end of the brilliant first period of the Israelite monarchy.

The history of the co-existence of 'Israel' in the north and 'Judah' in the south was marked at first by constant tension and indeterminate fighting on the frontier. From the time of Omri's reign (which began in 882 BC) the advantage lay with Israel. But about that time foreign powers began again to affect the destinies of both states. From the beginning of the ninth century the northern kingdom was involved in struggles with the Arameans. Only a little later the Assyrians began to push forward towards Syria; and to repel them Israel allied for the time being with the Arameans. In 841, when Shalmaneser III advanced as far as Damascus, Jehu of Israel had to pay him a heavy tribute.

In the following decades the Assyrians' pressure again slackened for a time; but this meant that Israel was once more menaced by the Arameans, till the latter's power was finally broken by the Assyrians. This enabled Israel again to experience something of a heyday in the first half of the eighth century. This, however, was abruptly ended by the plans for world conquest by Tiglath-pileser III (who ascended the throne in 745) and his successors. In 733 the Assyrians conquered Israel and turned its northern regions into Assyrian provinces; and finally in 722/21, after renewed anti-Assyrian resistance, they completely annihilated Israel's existence as a state and incorporated the whole of its territory in the Assyrian empire. The Israelite upper classes were deported, and groups of foreign populations from territories conquered by the Assyrians were settled there. It was not till centuries later that Galilee, the northern part of the country, regained any importance for the history of Israel.

The Kings of Israel

When the empire that David had created broke up after Solomon's death, the kings of the new states that replaced it were in strongly contrasted situations. The southern state, Judah, had two essential advantages that favoured a successful continuity in succession to the great epoch of the reign of David and Solomon. First, Rehoboam, the king of Judah, was a son of Solomon and therefore one of David's family. As a member of a dynasty that was already firmly established, he could continue the existing line; and no difficulties seem to have been raised in Judah itself on this question. Secondly, Jerusalem, the capital, was within the territory of Judah, even though it was close to the northern frontier. Here, during the long reign of the two great kings, there had developed an intellectual and religious centre whose leading role was by now beyond dispute, and which exercised a strong influence throughout Judah's territory. Dynasty and religious centre, joined together in Jerusalem, offered a firm foundation for the state's future.

Israel, the northern state, was quite a different matter. There the prerequisites for the new monarchy had first to be created, for it had no dynasty and no traditional official residence; and above all, it lacked an intellectual and religious centre. The northern state, however, developed along lines completely different from those indicated by the reigns of David and Solomon. The kings of Israel evidently made no serious attempt to create a royal residence that would at the same time be a great religious and cultic centre. We learn from I Kings that Jeroboam, the king of Israel, proceeded at once to set up new sanctuaries in the land; and indeed he bestowed a special status as state sanctuaries on two places with traditional cultic associations, near the northern and southern frontiers of the country. In the north the sanctuary was the city of Dan, which, according to tradition, had been built when the tribe of that name settled there. In the south a new importance came to Bethel, which could already look back over a long history that was particularly associated with the name of the patriarch Jacob.

The narrative in I Kings 12.26ff. expressly emphasizes that Jeroboam set up those two sanctuaries to prevent the people of his state from continuing their former practice of going to religious celebrations in the Jerusalem sanctuary. He was afraid – probably with good reason – that the religious appeal of Jerusalem might have political repercussions that would weaken his position in relation to the king of Judah. Those measures that he took are described as apostasy from the true faith, as an arbitrary action that was reprehensible on religious grounds; and indeed the subsequent accounts of the kings of Israel refer continually to the 'sins of Jeroboam', by which is meant the setting up of the sanctuaries. This represents the standpoint of Judah, or rather of Jerusalem, and is a basically negative judgment of Jeroboam's conduct. Of course, the measures taken by David and Solomon, who had given Jerusalem its religious significance by keeping the ark of the covenant there, and later by building the temple, had been well-considered and statesmanlike; and no one would then have denied the king's right to make such decisions about religious institutions. On the other hand, Jeroboam's cultic innovations actually involved a far-reaching interference in the religious tradition of the Israelites as a whole, and the consequences were bound to follow.

The cultic symbols that Jeroboam set up in Bethel and Dan are generally known now as 'golden calves'. But that description contains an element of depreciation, which again is determined by Jerusalem's critical point of view. The things in question were golden images of a bull, and their exact significance is even now uncertain. It is often assumed that the bull must be understood here as a symbol used in Canaanite worship, as the representative of a fertility cult as practised in the Canaanite religion. But the tradition, for all its polemical outlook, says nothing of this;

indeed, it connects the golden bulls directly with one specific element of the Israelite religion, namely the deliverance out of Egypt (I Kings 12.28). So it is not disputed that it was a question of Israelite worship, which means the worship of Yahweh; what is criticized is the competition with the sanctuary of Jerusalem. For that reason, too, it is unlikely that the golden bulls themselves were regarded as representing the deity, as that would hardly have been compatible with the religion of Yahweh. We must rather suppose that, as we know from numerous oriental pictures, they are to be thought of as pedestals on which the invisible Yahweh is standing; indeed, the ark of the covenant was one such throne of an invisible God.

Thus the new state had created its own sanctuaries, and at least that of Bethel was able to fulfil the role assigned to it as a state sanctuary, as we see, for instance, in the appearance there of the prophet Amos nearly two hundred years later. The history of the new royal residence was not quite such plain sailing. It seems that Jeroboam first chose as his capital Shechem, a famous old city which, like Bethel, was associated in the Israelite tradition with the patriarch Jacob and with Joshua, and which, moreover, was the natural centre of the northern part of the country. But he soon left that city, and went back for a time to Penuel east of the Jordan – a move probably connected with the invasion of the territory by the Pharaoh Shoshenk (Shishak in the biblical tradition). After that, he began to develop a new residence in Tirzah, a city to the north of Shechem. But even that did not become Israel's final capital, for a few years later King Omri decided to move the royal residence once again. But this time he did not follow existing traditions, but founded a completely new city, Samaria, on a hitherto unoccupied hill (I Kings 16.24).

Various causes may have contributed to this latest move. First, there were perhaps geographical reasons. Owing to its position, Tirzah looked out towards the east, towards Jordan and the territories to the east and north, whereas it lacked lines of communication towards the west. But it was an important part of the policy of Omri and his successors to cultivate good relations with the Phoenician coastal towns, and so he attached great importance to westward lines of communication. Besides this, it is particularly noteworthy that the city of Samaria achieved a very special status, comparable to that which David gave to Jerusalem. Like the latter, Samaria was an independent city-state, under the direct jurisdiction of the king and possessing its own rights. It is a striking fact here that in this capital of the kingdom of Israel there was a temple for the Canaanite god Baal, whereas we are told nothing about a sanctuary for the Israelite God Yahweh. It has been inferred from these special features in the situation of Samaria that Omri wished to create here for the Canaanites, who were relatively strong numerically in his own state, a place where they could live according to their own traditions. One thinks particularly here of the Canaanite 'nobility', whose business had always been to keep itself at the king's disposal for tasks connected with the court, the army, and the administration. So, in the time of Omri and his successors, the city of Samaria may have been greatly affected by the Canaanite way of life.

But although this question cannot now be decided with any certainty, it does touch on a very special problem that existed in the northern kingdom. Over wide stretches of that country the Israelites had settled down to peaceful coexistence with the Canaanites, and although the Israelites had clearly been the pre-dominant party since David's time, the Canaanite part of the population was still there; and that fact gave rise to political, and even more to religious problems. The latter played a particularly important part at the time of the prophet Elijah.

The tension existing in the northern kingdom is particularly evident in the fact that the history of the monarchy in Israel, side by side with these Canaanite elements, presents specifically Israelite characteristics. In Judah the dynastic idea had evidently taken root without opposition, and so the monarchy was in line with the usual practice in the ancient East; but Israel never produced a dynasty that really lasted. Among the counteracting forces that worked against the establishment of a dynasty, one must be specially emphasized – the prophets. According to tradition, a prophet played a decisive part at the very beginning of the separate northern monarchy, as it was Ahijah of Shiloh who designated Jeroboam as king while Solomon was still on the throne; and he may well have given the final impetus to Jeroboam's abortive attempt at revolution (I Kings 11.29ff.). The monarchy is regarded here as directly instituted by God. But that means at the same time that it has a direct responsibility towards God, and that the kingship can be revoked and certainly cannot be handed on at will. Even in Jeroboam's lifetime there was conflict between him and the prophet Ahijah; and when his son Nadab was the victim of a revolution soon after he had mounted the throne, it was regarded as the fulfilment of the judgment that the prophet had pronounced on him (I Kings 15.25ff.). When the narratives, which looked back from a later point of time, were compiled, they express a definite understanding of the role of prophecy – that is, of a divine participation in the appointment of kings in Israel.

This feature is again particularly stressed in the figure of the prophet Elisha. King Omri had succeeded in consolidating the Israelite monarchy once more, and his son Ahab successfully continued his policy. But it was under these two kings that the Canaanites' position within the northern kingdom grew stronger; and this gave rise to the protest by the prophets, who felt that here they were preserving the true Israelite tradition. The upshot was not only sharp disputes between Elijah and King Ahab, but also the destruction of the dynasty founded by Omri. According to the tradition in II Kings 9 and 10, it was the prophet Elisha who, again by secretly designating a new king, set off a revolution. At the instance of the prophet an officer of the king's army, Jehu by name, seized power. How important a part the religious element played here is shown by the first measures taken by Jehu. He had the temple of Baal in the royal city of Samaria demolished, and the Baal-worshippers who had gathered inside it slaughtered.

So the history of the monarchy in the northern kingdom had taken another decisive turn. King Jehu, who had come to power at the prophet's behest, was able to establish yet another dynasty, which in fact kept the throne in Samaria for nearly a century – a short time, it is true, compared with the more than four hundred years of the Davidic dynasty. The first half of the eighth century was a comparatively peaceful time during the long reign of Jeroboam II.

After the fall of Jehu's dynasty, the history of the northern kingdom was quickly finished. Weakened by internal confusion, and especially by frequent changes of the monarchy, the little state was soon drawn into the ferment in which the Assyrians' plans of world conquest involved the whole territory of Syria and Palestine. Desperate efforts were made to hold up the Assyrian invasion; in fact, with that object Israel even joined its hereditary enemies the Arameans in an anti-Assyrian coalition. But after only a short time the Assyrians had broken down all opposition. In 721 the city of Samaria fell after a siege lasting three years, and with that the doom of the northern kingdom was sealed; the state that went by the official name of Israel ceased to exist, and its land became an Assyrian province. The history of the nation of Israel, however, was continued in Judah, where Jerusalem in particular was to remain the supremely important focal point for the future.

Thus in the two hundred years' history of the kings of Israel there was no lack of tension. As regards the individual kings, a special difficulty in the way of forming a sound judgment lies in the nature of the tradition in the Old Testament Books of Kings. Anyone who reads these texts will very soon notice that their real interest is not in presenting the historical events, and that they are not concerned to evaluate the kings' political and military achievements. It is only from time to time that events and courses of action are described in detail. But the narratives nearly always centre on the king and on the disputes that occur between him and a prophet; in fact, most of the more detailed narratives about a king are really narratives about a prophet. They were not composed by writers of history or by chroniclers whose aim was to ascertain the exact course of events; on the contrary, they originated in, and were handed on by, prophetic circles in which the real object of interest was the role of the prophet. That

60

means that the picture of the king was nearly always illuminated from one particular angle.

There is even stronger evidence of a particular way of regarding the monarchy in the brief remarks that are made at the beginning and end of a king's reign: the kings are judged there almost exclusively by religious standards. In the case of all the kings of the northern kingdom we are told that they walked in the 'sins' of Jeroboam by allowing the sanctuaries of Bethel and Dan to exist. So that the final judgment on them is always negative. This outlook was finally summarized retrospectively in a review of the entire history of the northern kingdom in II Kings 17. That history is there presented as a history of the defection from Yahweh, the God of Israel, and so the fate of the northern kingdom appears as the inevitable consequence of that sin. Obviously there were other sources of information about the kings' activities; for in the concluding remarks on the reign of each king we are told that everything else about him is recorded in the 'Book of the Chronicles of the Kings of Israel' (or 'of Judah'). Unfortunately we no longer have those sources, because the interest of the people who compiled or edited the Books of Kings, and gave them their final form, was a different one.

We must therefore try to understand two things: the kings' policy and achievements on the one hand, and the purpose of this obviously one-sided historical writing on the other. No doubt the kings of Israel included some impressive figures: Jeroboam I, who founded the new state and created the conditions necessary for what followed; Omri, the far-sighted founder of the new royal residence Samaria, who, like his son Ahab, had striking achievements to his credit, both in a prudent foreign policy and in extensive building activities that have been brought to light by archaeological research; Jehu, who with his changed internal policy laid the foundation for a stabilization of relationships that enabled the dynasty that he founded to maintain itself on the throne for a century; Jeroboam II, under whom Israel once more flourished for the last time. All these kings, as well as others of less importance, certainly did their best to carry out the tasks that their office imposed on them.

We might therefore be inclined to draw a 'purely historical' picture of these kings, and to dismiss the narratives in the Books of Kings as biased and tendentious. But on the other hand, we have to ask how this negative picture originated. We have already seen that there were certain definite problems that ran like a scarlet thread through those two centuries. Above all, there was the question of the relationship between the Israelite and the Canaanite traditions. It is understandable, and it may have been wise from the point of view of internal politics, that the kings – especially Omri and Ahab – gave the Canaanite elements more scope and tried to maintain a kind of equilibrium between the two. But by doing so they necessarily came into conflict with the first principles of the Israelite religion, which had been the common basis of all the Israelite tribes since the time of their federation. It was a conflict between Israel's religious fundamentals (which, however, had never been merely 'religious' in a purely private and personal sense, but from early times had formed a uniting bond for all Israelites) on the one hand, and 'reasons of state' on the other. It is not possible for us today to judge how the kings could or ought to have behaved; but we have to admit, on any estimate, that they were not able to resolve the conflict.

The northern kingdom's assertion of cultic independence raises similar problems. No doubt there was a political advantage in severing the cultic ties with Jerusalem. On the other hand, it is probable that in the long reigns of David and Solomon the significance of Jerusalem as the intellectual and religious centre of all Israel had so sunk into the general consciousness that no such severance could take place without endangering historical continuity. For that reason, the criticism of Jeroboam's measures was probably not inspired simply by a selfish local patriotism of Jerusalem; the matter involved very serious problems which constantly bedevilled the history of the northern kingdom. As far as we can tell from the Old Testament tradition, there were circles there which, being very conscious of the Israelite traditions, cultivated them and tried to make them effective. But they seem mostly to have been in opposition to the official state policy, as we see especially in the behaviour of the prophets.

Thus the negative picture that the Books of Kings draw of the Israelite kings brings out problems that were actually present throughout that state's history. The conflict between the genuinely Israelite traditions and the political decisions of the kings remains as an unresolved tension over the history of the northern kingdom.

The history of prophecy forms an important part of the history of Israel. At the time of Saul and David – that is, round about 1000 BC – there appear the first prophetic figures that can be grasped historically. During the tenth century the tradition mentions prophets several times, for example Ahijah of Shiloh, who set up Jeroboam as King of Israel. The history of prophecy reaches its first climax about the middle of the ninth century in Elijah and Elisha.

Elijah's appearance is closely connected with the religious policy of King Ahab (871-852), who deliberately furthered the Canaanite element in Israel. In this he was supported by his wife Jezebel, who was the daughter of a Phoenician (and so a 'Canaanite') king.

Elijah

The prophets are among the most important and yet the most peculiar figures of Old Testament history. They appear on the scene repeatedly from the beginning of the monarchy, especially in times of internal or external tensions and crises. For all that, the phenomenon of Israelite prophecy is by no means uniform; on the contrary, it raises a whole series of questions, some of which have not even yet been answered by scholarly research.

One of the first questions as to how we are to understand prophecy arises at once from the outward circumstances of the prophets' appearance. They often appear as detached and even solitary people, like Elijah, for instance. But side by side with this, we hear time and again of groups of prophets, of an almost corporate type; and at least some of the prophets who appeared singly were obviously connected with those groups in some definite way; we are expressly told this about Elisha, the pupil and disciple of Elijah. How are we to regard that relationship of the individual prophets to the groups? That is not a superficial question; it touches the fundamental problem how we are to understand prophecy in general. For it seems that the prophets who act individually become prophets through the divine call, and realize that they are responsible only to that call and to their own conscience, whereas a prophetic group necessarily assumes a certain tradition and continuity – indeed, the prophetic office here seems to be almost an occupation. Are we faced here with an opposition between things that are mutually exclusive? This question has been very vigorously discussed in recent research, and we shall probably have to come to the conclusion that we are not dealing here with a real antithesis. It is evident that there was in Israel a relatively stable institution of group prophecy, which probably devoted itself particularly to cultivating and preserving the traditions that came from the early days of the Israelite religion. But side by side with this there repeatedly appeared individual prophets, who, while they stood out from the group because of their special call, and often did not even have direct contact with it, yet shared with it as their basis the central religious traditions of Israel.

Here we have touched on a vital point. The prophets are not innovators or revolutionaries, but in a very high degree defenders and guardians of the old traditions. The opposition that is often apparent between them and their contemporaries arises from the fact that they are resisting certain developments that threaten to destroy Israel's basic traditions.

That can already be seen in the first great prophetic figure, who appeared in northern Israel about the middle of the ninth century BC, Elijah. If we survey the tradition about him that has come down to us, one dominant feature stands out clearly – the question at issue is the relationship between the Israelite and the Canaanite tradition. Thus the central problem of the state of Israel at that time is also Elijah's essential theme, and in dealing with it he shows himself a resolute and determined opponent of the royal policy all along the line. The texts give us the impression that it was not till Elijah came on the scene that the problems became sharply defined and so were forced on the general consciousness. The coexistence of the two civilizations and religions was no doubt so much taken for granted that their incompatibility was no longer felt.

It was natural that the religious sphere was the one where the opposition first became serious. On the occasion of a drought, Elijah declared that only Yahweh, the God of Israel, could give the hoped-for rain, and that people were not to expect it, as they generally did, from the Canaanite god Baal. And he announced divine punishment of King Ahaziah, Ahab's successor, because when he was ill he sought help from the god Baalzebub who was worshipped in the Philistines' town of Ekron, instead of from the God of Israel.

But the acute nature of the conflict comes out with special

force in the great narrative of Elijah's clash with the prophets of Baal on Mount Carmel, related in I Kings 18. Here was a problem that seemed to be of only local significance: there were on Mount Carmel a ruined altar of the Israelite God Yahweh, and an altar of Baal intact beside it. Presumably there were historical-political reasons for their being side by side, because Carmel was in the border territory between Israel and the neighbouring Phoenicians, and the place had changed hands several times. In Ahab's time the Israelites were again in possession; but in spite of this, the god Baal was still worshipped there, and Baal was in a somewhat different form the Phoenicians' god. Elijah intended to put an end to that state of affairs, and he challenged the prophets of Baal – the tradition gives their number as four hundred and fifty – to a divine judgment. Each side was to prepare a sacrifice but put no fire to it; and then each was to pray to its god to send down fire from heaven; and the result was to decide which of the two gods was the real God. The narrative relates that the prayers of the prophets of Baal had no success, but that in response to Elijah's prayer fire came down from heaven and consumed his sacrifice. That, it is said, convinced the people that Yahweh, the God of Israel, was the true God.

We can see here that Elijah saw the two religions, which had so far existed side by side, as alternatives: Yahweh or Baal. And we can also see that he made the cultic problem, which may have seemed to be a local one on Mount Carmel, a fundamental question for all Israel. But in view of King Ahab's religious policy, this was a challenge which was aggravated by the fact that his consort Jezebel was a Phoenician king's daughter who devoted herself particularly to cultivating the Canaanite elements in Israel. So there was bound to develop an implacable hostility between Elijah and the royal house.

But the conflict was concerned, not only with the religious sphere in the narrower sense, but also with the position of the king in relation to his subjects. In this connection we are told that Ahab forcibly took possession of the vineyard of an Israelite named Naboth who would not sell it to him, and whom he therefore got rid of by judicial murder. Here we see two quite different legal conceptions opposed to each other: on the one hand the old Israelite agrarian law, which provided that real estate was to remain within the family and was inalienable, because, strictly speaking, the God of Israel himself was the land-owner and had merely handed it over to the Israelites for their use; and on the other hand the ideas of an absolute monarchy with the basic right to dispose even of its subjects' property. Here, too, Elijah came on the scene and told the king that God would punish him for his conduct. Again, this intensified the opposition between the king and the prophet.

In all these disputes Elijah is represented as a vehement and fearless man, willing to stand alone against the King and against the whole nation. To his contemporaries there must indeed have been something uncanny about him. He suddenly appears where he is least expected; and once we are actually told (in II Kings 1) that detachments of soldiers who were to arrest him were destroyed by fire that came down from heaven. So the figure of Elijah bursts all human bounds, as it were.

But the tradition shows us the other side, too. When Jezebel threatens to kill him, Elijah flees into the desert (I Kings 19). There, despairing of his mission and of Israel's future, he sits down under a broom tree and asks that he may die – according to the ideas of ancient Israel a very wrong thought, and one that expresses the utter loneliness of that great solitary figure. But here, too, God does not abandon him. On the mountain in the desert, where God had revealed himself to Moses long ago, he now reveals himself to Elijah, too.

This puts Elijah's life work into a larger context. He had been made the messenger of God's judgment on the people of Israel, who had turned to the worship of a strange god. Now it appears that others after him will carry out that judgment – the Arameans, who will beset Israel from without, and the usurper Jehu, who will liquidate the existing ruling dynasty in Israel. Here we meet for the first time such a view of history as became characteristic of the entire line of great prophetic figures after Elijah: Israel is God's people. But that implies not only a privilege, but above all a special obligation; and if Israel withdraws from that obligation, it will have to bear the consequences in the form of historical catastrophes. All this illustrates very impressively that in Israelite thought religion is not merely a matter of contemplation, but penetrates right down into the people's life and determines its destiny.

But something else is brought out in the account of God's appearing to Elijah. The judgment is proclaimed, but at the same time it is said that not all will be doomed by it; a remnant will remain in Israel: seven thousand, 'all the knees that have not bowed to Baal, and every mouth that has not kissed him'. That, too, is a thought that runs through the whole history of prophecy: that in the catastrophe a remnant will be left, with whom the history of God's dealings with his people will continue to take its course. For that was, in fact, a problem that was bound to cause the prophets constant thought and grief. They were deeply convinced that God had a very special purpose for Israel, and yet they themselves had to proclaim God's judgment to the nation. From that proclamation of judgment they could omit nothing; but again and again the conviction came to them that this was not the last word on Israel's destiny, but that there would always be a fresh start, even if it were only with a small remnant that survived the catastrophe.

In all this, Elijah appears as the forerunner of a line of prophets in the following centuries. Above all, he was the first to realize that Israel could not serve two masters. His contemporaries remembered him as a figure of unique greatness, and his image was finally elevated into the miraculous. It was said that he did not die a natural death, but that, before the eyes of Elisha, his disciple and successor in prophecy, he was taken up to heaven in a chariot of fire. His figure surpassed human limits, and so in the last resort it could not be measured by human standards.

About the middle of the eighth century BC there again emerges in the Old Testament tradition a line of significant prophetic figures. The oldest of them is Amos, who appeared, as did his slightly younger contemporary Hosea, in the northern kingdom of Israel. He was active during the time of King Jeroboam II (787-747), under whose reign the northern kingdom once again experienced a time of external peace and internal stability.

Amos

About a century after Elijah, we again hear of the appearance of a line of prophets. There is now a striking change in the outward form of tradition. About the older prophets we are given longer or shorter narratives in which their actual words do not bulk very large. Now, however, we have whole collections of prophetic utterances from which quite often there emerge no details of the relevant circumstances in which they were delivered. The interest has therefore clearly shifted to the message itself.

The result of that shift is that while we are to a large extent very well informed about the prophets' words and thoughts, we do not know much about their personal lives and destinies. It is not till we come to the later prophets, especially Jeremiah, that these personal matters again become more prominent.

The first in the line of eighth-century prophets is Amos, of whom we learn that he was a shepherd from Tekoa, a small town to the south of Jerusalem. But this information promptly confronts us with a curious difficulty. Amos appears as a prophet, and claims to speak in God's name; but when the priest Amaziah takes the matter up with him at the Bethel sanctuary, he repudiates the title of prophet: 'I am no prophet, nor a prophet's son; but I am a herdsman, and a dresser of sycamore trees' (7.14). Here we again see the strained relations that existed, or at any rate might arise at any time, between the prophetic groups and the individual prophets acting separately. Although in principle there was no opposition between them, and although there were even intermittent close contacts between prophetic groups and certain individual prophets, yet the groups might be repeatedly drawn into the interplay of forces of the various religious and religio-political currents in Israel, whereas the distinguishing characteristic of the prophets who acted alone was their independence.

Amos, therefore, protests against his opponent's attempted classification, and appeals solely to the direct divine commission that he has received: 'The Lord took me from following the flock, and the Lord said to me, "Go, prophesy to my people Israel." ' He has been commissioned as a prophet, not through belonging to a certain group or corporate body, but directly through a divine command that he could not evade. We cannot now re-enact the inward processes of such a prophet's calling; but from Amos' words we still get some idea of the elemental and inescapable power that met him, when he says (3.8): 'The lion has roared; who will not fear? The Lord God has spoken; who can but prophesy?'

The whole of Amos' words and demeanour conveys something of that elemental force and of the inescapable nature of what has been laid upon him, which he has to pass on. He is perhaps the most thorough-going 'prophet of judgment' among all the Old Testament prophets. And he faces fearlessly and unswervingly, with his message of disaster, the public opinion of all Israel, as well as the king himself. In this respect he clearly resembles Elijah.

The message about the royal house caused particular offence. Amos appeared with his prophecy at the state sanctuary in Bethel, probably on the occasion of one of the great pilgrimage festivals that were celebrated there, at which a great crowd of people would gather. It was no unusual thing in Israel for a prophet to come forward at such a festival; it may even be that prophetic messages formed a regular part of the programme. And it is not out of the question that critical voices were repeatedly raised, foretelling disaster, and that the prophets called on the assembled people to turn from their wrong ways and think back to the fundamentals of their faith. But Amos obviously went too far. He announced an imminent and inescapable disaster for the whole of Israel – one that had been ordained by none other than Israel's God himself as the inescapable consequence of his people's own conduct. And he told the people with terrible directness, in the form of a direct word from God (7.9): 'I will rise against the house of Jeroboam with the sword.'

That was bound to be interpreted as open rebellion against the king. Amaziah the priest, who was evidently responsible for the state sanctuary in Bethel, reported those outrageous goings-on to the king, at the same time ordering the prophet to leave the country. Expositors are not agreed on whether that indicated a hostile attitude towards Amos, or whether the priest wanted to protect him from prosecution by the king, and therefore counselled flight, after he had dutifully reported the matter. In any case, Amos found the demand unacceptable, as, of course, he saw in it an attempt to prevent him from carrying out the commission that he had received from God. So he replied with a caustic judgment on the priest himself, and renewed his prophecy of Israel's doom.

We are told nothing about the upshot of this dispute, nor do we know how long Amos continued his prophetic activity. Some scholars think that it extended only over that particular festival – perhaps, indeed, only over a single day. But even though all these questions remain unsolved, we can recognize quite clearly the outlines of his prophetic message.

Like all the prophets, Amos was no innovator; on the contrary, he stood out as an upholder of the ancient Israelite traditions. Indeed, in many cases he thought them out so consistently and logically that his final conclusions were exactly the opposite of those to which the people of that time were accustomed. One point, which he brings out very clearly and sharply, was felt by his contemporaries to be very important in relation to their consciousness of being in a special way chosen by God. Amos takes up this article of belief in a surprising way: 'You only have I known of all the families of the earth; therefore I will punish you all for all your iniquities', runs the divine message (3.2). He affirms Israel's special position before God; and he does not infer from it, as was probably usual among the Israelites of his time, that it gave them special privileges and the perpetual certainty of divine mercy and protection regardless of their own conduct; instead, he regards the 'election' as bringing special obligation and responsibility before God. It is precisely because of its special position that God will judge Israel by special standards. And how far Amos is from accepting the idea of a privileged position of Israel in relation to other nations is clear from the passage in chapter 9: ' "Are you not like the Ethiopians to me, O people of Israel?" says the Lord. "Did I not bring up Israel from the land of Egypt, and the Philistines from Caphtor and the Syrians from Kir?" ' God has led other nations, too; and Amos does not concede to Israel the right, on the ground of its historical experience of God's guidance, to consider itself any better than the other nations. Here he formulated a basic idea of Israel's religious tradition in a new and striking way, so that it was bound to seem to his contemporaries like a negation of the traditional ideas. He brought the idea of Israel's election back into what, in view of its essential nature, is its only rightful place – into the sphere of the relationship between God and Israel; and he resolutely contested its right to political extension.

On another point, too, Amos deals in like manner with the tradition. On the strength of old traditional ideas, Israel expected an appointed day on which God would openly reveal his power. This 'day of Yahweh' was popularly understood to mean the final victory of Israel over its enemies, and was therefore awaited as a day of rejoicing. But again Amos denounces any such view: 'Woe to you who desire the day of the Lord! Why would you have the day of the Lord? It is darkness, and not light'; and in a depressing picture he describes the inevitability of the calamity that that day will bring: 'As if a man fled from a lion, and a bear met him; or went into the house and leaned with his hand against the wall, and a serpent bit him' (5.19). In contrast to the prevailing self-satisfied optimism, Amos gives an entirely different picture of the manifestation of God's power – a picture that is to call the people to self-critical vigilance.

There is one more theme that stands out very clearly in the Book of Amos. Some of the sharpest shafts of his criticism are aimed at the sphere that we should now call 'social'. He reproaches the Israelites with oppressing and exploiting the poor; with living on the fat of the land at the expense of the poor; with acting unjustly towards widows and orphans who cannot themselves assert their legal claims; with making dishonest gains by false weights and other shady devices; with perverting justice by bribery and by influencing witnesses. All these reproaches are clearly directed against a certain class of rich people; and it has been supposed that they express the social sense of the simple unspoilt man of the people in relation to conditions in the large towns. But the roots of the criticism go deeper. The demands for right and justice, for care for the poor, the widows, and the orphans, form part of the oldest bases of Israelite law. And they are to be found in those very parts of the Old Testament legal code which contain specifically Israelite traditions. It may well be supposed that on certain occasions they were solemnly read out in divine service, so that people actually spoke of a 'law of God'. So we can see again that Amos is not making new social demands here, but that he is holding up to the Israelites their own basic traditions, with a consistency that had quite escaped his contemporaries, as a standard by which to judge their actions.

All this goes to show that the prophets are always concerned with quite concrete problems of their own time. The time during which Amos appeared was one of calm in foreign affairs, and so of stability in home affairs. The long reign of Jeroboam II was one of the most peaceful and perhaps prosperous periods in the history of the northern kingdom. But that period, too, had evidently seen a shifting of social relationships in Israel. Whereas previously all Israelite citizens had had their share of landed property for the support of themselves and their families, there had now developed, partly through the expansion of trade, and partly perhaps through a definite policy of the kings in relation to ownership, a class of property-owners who tended to increase their wealth more and more at other people's expense, and who in doing so evidently did not shrink from underhand means and callous practices. So, as a negative consequence of the favourable external situation, the foundations of Israel's social life were threatened with destruction.

Against this the prophet Amos directed his biting criticism. The social order had from time immemorial been one of the essentials of the Israelite religion; and one of its pillars was faith in God's covenant with Israel. That covenant, however, established a close social relationship within the community, and those two aspects of the covenant were inseparable. Thus any disintegration of the social order endangered at the same time the fundamentals of Israel's religion, and therefore its vital root.

Amos was one of the first to realize the danger, and he took the strongest possible stand against it. Today, when we try to take in the full force of his words, we are startled by the finality with which they proclaim the divine judgment. We are conscious that we can no longer penetrate the secret of the prophetic self-confidence that they express. But we recognize in Amos one of the great figures of the Israelite religion who helped to fashion its image and to make it a vital force through the centuries.

For a long time the state of Judah stood in the shadow of the more powerful Israel; but the kings of Omri's dynasty ended the hostilities between the two states and made the kings of Judah their allies. We read several times of campaigns undertaken jointly, and at last King Jehoram of Judah even married the daughter of Ahab of Israel.

In the last decades of the state of Israel, Judah was drawn into the unrest caused by the advance of the Assyrians when, in 733, the Israelite king, in common with the Arameans, tried to force King Ahaz of Judah to join an anti-Assyrian coalition; but Ahaz appealed to the Assyrians for help, and so became their vassal. His successor Hezekiah tried to get rid of the Assyrian domination; but in 701 he had to pay a heavy tribute to the Assyrian King Sennacherib, who was besieging Jerusalem.

The downfall of Assyria enabled Judah for a short time to consolidate and extend its political power, and Josiah in particular (639-609) used the opportunity. But the rise of the Babylonian empire, in succession to the Assyrian, meant the end of the state of Judah. In 597 the Babylonian king Nebuchadnezzar conquered Jerusalem and took King Jehoiachin and some of the leading members of the community into exile in Babylon. When resistance to the Babylonians was renewed, Nebuchadnezzar besieged Jerusalem in 587 for the second time, destroyed it, and brought Judah's independence to an end. For the following centuries it remained a province under the domination of one or other of the great powers.

The Kings of Judah

When the Israelite empire that David had created broke up after Solomon's death, the rulers of the northern kingdom had to find a new basis for their monarchy. But in the southern kingdom, Judah, the kings were able to continue, without a break, what they had inherited from their great predecessors. For, on the one hand, the long reigns of David and Solomon had apparently made it seem almost a matter of course that the Davidic dynasty should continue to reign in Jerusalem; and on the other hand there already existed in Jerusalem an intellectual and religious centre whose pre-eminence could no longer be questioned.

In this connection, the special situation in Jerusalem gave the monarchy there a peculiarly twofold character. David had, indeed, occupied Jerusalem, up to then inhabited by Canaanites, and had made it his personal residence; and so he had added to his double kingship of Judah and Israel the kingship of the city of Jerusalem. This kingship, however, had cultic roots that went back a long way, and David apparently took these over and entered into the existing traditional setting. The memory of Jerusalem's pre-Israelite royal tradition is particularly associated with the figure of Melchizedek, of whom we are told in Genesis 14 that Abraham met him and paid him tribute. Melchizedek is described as holding a twofold office: he is 'king of Salem' (Jerusalem) and 'priest of God Most High'. So this union of kingship and priesthood, which often occurred in the ancient East, seems also to have existed in the city-kingdom of Jerusalem in pre-Israelite times. And David entered on this twofold office. In Psalm 110 there is handed down to us the liturgy for a festival at which David himself or one of his successors was installed in the kingly-priestly office. First it speaks of sovereign authority being conferred, when it says: 'The Lord says to my lord: "Sit at my right hand, till I make your enemies your footstool."' And after that, a divine oath to the king is renewed: '"You are a priest for ever after the order of Melchizedek."' Kingship and priesthood, both bestowed by Yahweh, characterize the Jerusalem monarchy.

It is plain here from the wording of this psalm that its outlook is not simply on the immediate state of affairs, but that it is meant to give a definite picture of Jerusalem monarchy: the king is the world-ruler appointed by God. We can see this still more clearly in other psalms; in Psalm 2, for instance, we read that God himself has set his king on Zion, his holy hill, and that the attempts of the other kings of the earth to seize the mastery for themselves are therefore predestined to failure. The close conjunction of the king with God is made very clear by his announcing a divine decision in the liturgical setting of his accession to the throne: 'He said to me, "You are my son, today I have begotten you."' The king is therefore understood to be God's 'son' – not, indeed, in the physical sense as was usual in Egypt, but figuratively, in that when the king mounted the throne he was installed as God's 'son'. The statement that God has begotten the king is meant here in a figurative sense, for the 'today' is the day of enthronement on which the king took over his rights and duties.

Finally, there are in some psalms expressions that elevate the picture of the king into the realm of the miraculous. It is said of him in Psalm 72 that during his reign the land is blessed with paradisal fertility, and even that he will live as long as the sun and moon shine. These are the features of an idealized king who stands quite outside human realities – the kind of thing that we find in other civilizations of the ancient East. It is not easy to say how this conception of the king found its way into the Israelite religion. Some scholars see in it 'messianic' features describing a king who will not appear until the time of salvation in the last days. Others would relate this messianic element to the present, assigning the king a place that lies outside the human realm and gives him participation in the divine sphere. But these questions can no longer be decided with any certainty, as we have in the Psalms only the liturgical texts without any explanatory material.

In any case, all this shows us only one side of the Jerusalem monarchy – the internal, cultic side, which assimilated many elements from the pre- and extra-Israelite religious tradition. And one has to ask how far 'outside' in the land of Judah these things were known and realized. For there are other quite different features in the picture of the monarchy. It is evident, not only that the Davidic dynasty was an accepted historical fact, but that the people of Judah outside Jerusalem seem to have taken a keen interest in its fortunes, and to have shown themselves ready to champion the rights of the royal house.

Only once did there come a break in the line of kings from the house of David; but even that incident only shows how firmly the idea that the Davidic dynasty should rule as a matter of course had taken root in the national consciousness. It was the time when Judah had formed a particularly close link with Israel, the two royal houses even emphasizing their union through a political marriage: Athaliah, the daughter of King Ahab of Israel, became the wife of the Crown Prince of Judah, later King Jehoram. But this involved Judah in the internal political troubles of the northern kingdom. Ahaziah of Judah, who had meantime become king in succession to his father Jehoram, was on a visit to Israel when he fell victim to Jehu's revolution (II Kings 9.27). Athaliah, wishing to avenge her son, seized power in Judah, and succeeded in holding it for six years. But then the tradition-conscious circles in Judah rallied again; by a sudden coup they put on the throne the seven-year-old Joash, the only surviving son of Ahaziah, and so put an end to the interlude of Athaliah's reign (II Kings 11). In this the priests, the royal bodyguard, and the people of Jerusalem and Judah co-operated; they were evidently all of one mind on the question of the legal right of the Davidic monarchy.

Thus the monarchy of Judah was marked by stability and continuity. During the reign of many of the kings there was an obvious absence of special events and changes that might have been noted in the texts that have come down to us, so that we know little about them beyond the duration of their reign. It is only at a few focal points of the political scene that individual figures come more clearly into view; and on those occasions we see that, as with the kings of Israel, an important part is played by a prophet.

That is especially true of the time of the Assyrian menace, when the prophet Isaiah several times came into the forefront of events. For Judah the Assyrian advance at first represented an indirect danger. Its northern neighbours, Israel and the Aramean city of Damascus, had formed a coalition to call a halt to the Assyrians' march of conquest; and they tried to get the smaller neighbouring states to join them. But King Ahaz, who was then ruling in Jerusalem, opposed them. The kings of Israel and Aram then marched against Jerusalem, to compel him to join the coalition, or else to replace him by another king who would join it.

Isaiah 7 relates how Isaiah exhorted the frightened king to keep calm and rely on God's help. But Ahaz preferred to ask the Assyrians for help and to submit to them as their vassal by paying a heavy tribute. That enabled him to save his own monarchy, and for a time to keep the state of Judah intact; but in return for this he had to eat humble pie before the Assyrians. After a meeting in Damascus with the Assyrian King Tiglath-pileser III (II Kings 16.10), and no doubt on the latter's insistence, he had an Assyrian altar set up in Jerusalem. It was in line with ancient oriental custom that the victor also claimed a suitable place for his own state cult in the chief sanctuary of the vanquished; and Ahaz had to conform to the demand.

In the reign of his son and successor Hezekiah, the union of foreign policy and cultic changes turned at first in the opposite direction. When, a few decades later, he tried to throw off the Assyrian domination, he got rid at the same time of the foreign cultic objects in the temple at Jerusalem. But he had to pay dearly for his efforts at independence. The Assyrian King Sennacherib occupied the whole land of Judah with his troops and besieged Jerusalem, so that Hezekiah again had to submit to him and pay a heavy tribute. The fact that the city itself was not destroyed was regarded by its inhabitants as a miracle, although in fact it meant the complete shipwreck of Hezekiah's policy.

It is probable that Hezekiah himself had to restore the Assyrian cult in Jerusalem. In the tradition as recorded in the Books of Kings (II Kings 21), his son Manasseh is particularly blamed for allowing and promoting such a thing in the temple. For during his long reign (it lasted more than half a century) there was no change in Israel's status as Assyria's vassal, and so the Assyrian cult kept its place in the temple at Jerusalem.

It was not till the last third of the seventh century that historical conditions once again made it possible for the state of Judah to develop independently. Throughout the centuries, the destiny of Israel and its two constituent kingdoms had been determined repeatedly by the changing interplay of forces of foreign great powers. David's empire was able to originate in a period when Egypt's centuries-old predominance in the Syria-Palestine area had come to an end, and the Assyrians had not yet made good their claims to the territory. Later it was more than once the relaxation of the Assyrian grip that brought a breathing-space and possibilities of limited development. Then, in the second half of the seventh century, the Assyrian power drew towards its end. The Babylonians, who after a time of great power had then for a long while been dominated by the Assyrians, asserted their independence, and soon put an end to the great Assyrian empire. But in the interval before they could take over the full extent of the heritage of Assyria, there came once again a breathing-space for the states that had hitherto been vassals of the Assyrians.

In Judah the events of that time are associated with the name of Josiah, perhaps the most independent and clearly defined figure among the kings of Judah. He was a minor when he acceded to the throne; and his accession shows once again, as does that of the young boy Joash almost exactly two hundred years earlier, how intent the people of Judah were on maintaining the legitimate rule of the Davidic kings. They crushed a

83

revolt to which King Amon fell a victim, and Josiah, the murdered man's son, was made king at the age of eight (II Kings 21.23f.).

His religious reforms are described in detail in the Old Testament tradition as being the most important event of his reign. But as in the case of his predecessors, Josiah associated his religious changes with political measures. He could now safely and finally break away from the power of Assyria, and there followed the removal from the Jerusalem temple of Assyrian and other foreign forms of worship. But he was not content merely to restore his political independence within the state of Judah, for he seems to have succeeded in advancing a long way northwards into the territory of what had been the state of Israel, which had in the meantime become an Assyrian province. So, for the first time since the death of Solomon, a considerable part of essentially Israelite territory in what had been David's empire was reunited under a common rule. Josiah seems to have worked towards this aim consciously and consistently; he wanted to re-establish the kingdom of David.

Among his religious reforms, one is specially noteworthy. It is recorded that he broke down the 'high places'; that means that he abolished all the local sanctuaries apart from Jerusalem. Thus the temple in Jerusalem became the only legitimate sanctuary for the Israelite worship of Yahweh. According to II Kings 22 and 23, these measures were directly connected with a unique event. When the temple was being renovated, a 'book of the law' was found there, in which certain religious demands were laid down as divine instructions. According to the narrative, this produced the religious reforms. This book of the law obviously refers to Deuteronomy, or perhaps to an earlier version of it. For the demand that there should be only one sanctuary for the worship of the God of Israel is a central theme of the book. Its origin is not made quite clear, nor can we answer with any certainty the question how it got into the temple. It was evidently the work of a certain group of people in Israel who devoted themselves to collecting and handing on the essential religious traditions of their nation. They had probably written down their traditions at a time when they saw their continued existence threatened. Now, through Josiah, their work came into its own.

These religious reforms were of far-reaching importance. It is true that ever since the time of David and Solomon Jerusalem had had a place of its own in religious matters; but there had always been, in tradition, a larger or smaller number of other sanctuaries at which the Israelite God Yahweh was worshipped on cultic lines. But from the time of Josiah's reform Jerusalem became the only legitimate place for such worship. In spite of a counter-movement by his successors, this idea was very soon accepted; and from the time of the Babylonian exile Israel had no other sanctuary. This idea, too, had a marked effect on history-writing. For the final version of the Books of Kings used, as a yardstick for epochs long past, the demand for the exclusive rights of Jerusalem in this respect, and so passed very definite retrospective judgments on the kings.

But Josiah's ambitious and successful work was to come to an abrupt end. As the Babylonian power went on increasing, the Egyptians suddenly intervened. They preferred a weak Assyrian empire to a strong Babylonian one, and so they tried to keep the Assyrian power from complete collapse. For that purpose Pharaoh Neco marched north with an army in the year 609. Josiah saw in this a threat to his plans, and faced Neco at Megiddo in the north of his country. It does not seem, however, to have got as far as a battle, for we are told in II Kings 23.29 that 'Pharaoh Neco slew him at Megiddo, when he saw him.' With that, everything that Josiah had begun was finished with one blow.

For now the great powers renewed their attacks on the land of Judah. First the Egyptians were able to bring it under their rule for a short time. But they soon had to give way to the Babylonians, who here, too, took over the Assyrian empire; so Judah became a Babylonian vassal-state. King Jehoiakim tried once more to shake off the foreign yoke. But the Babylonian King Nebuchadnezzar soon put an end to that. He occupied Jerusalem, and took into exile in Babylon King Jehoiachin (who shortly before had succeeded his father, who had died during the siege) together with some of the leading citizens and certain groups of artisans. He did, indeed, leave in Jerusalem a monarchy dependent on himself; but when King Zedekiah again tried to break free from the Babylonian domination, Nebuchadnezzar marched on Jerusalem a second time and occupied it. This time he destroyed the city and carried off another section of the population to Babylon.

The last information that we are given in the tradition about a king of Judah is at the end of II Kings, where we are told that the Babylonian king released Jehoiachin from prison, allowed him to dine regularly at the king's table, and gave him a regular allowance as long as he lived. A chance find in Babylon has produced tablets of cuneiform writing of that period, recording deliveries of food to Jehoiachin and his attendants. So the story of the Kings of Judah ends with the figure of a prisoner at a foreign court.

In the history given us by the Books of Kings, the kings of both Judah and Israel are subjected to a retrospective judgment, whose standard is again an entirely religious one. But whereas the judgment on the kings of Israel is negative throughout, that on the kings of Judah is predominantly positive. Only certain small groups of kings are condemned because of their religious attitude – Jehoram and Ahaziah, for instance, who in the middle of the ninth century allied themselves closely with the royal house of Israel; Ahaz and Manasseh, who conceded a place in Jerusalem for the Assyrian state religions; and Josiah's successors who, instead of continuing his reforms, restored the earlier conditions.

In the positive judgments expressed on the remaining kings, there stands out one decisive standard – the figure of King David. Only a few kings get the highest commendation, namely that their conduct had been like that of their ancestor David; and among them are Hezekiah and Josiah, the two kings who had undertaken religious reforms during their reign. In one case, that of Amaziah (II Kings 14.3), it is said, by way of limitation, that his conduct was pleasing to God, but that it did not quite match that of David. And we are also told on one occasion (in I Kings

11), that God preserved the Jerusalem monarchy for David's sake. We can see here how the picture of David, the king after God's heart, was strong enough to impress itself on posterity, so that the whole of the succeeding epoch could be seen and judged historically by his standards. So, for all its inadequacy with regard to detail, the history of the monarchy of Judah is described in relation to the great example of this one king, whose name is at the same time bound up with the hopes of a final time of salvation in which a new David will make God's reign on earth a reality.

It is not till after the middle of the eighth century BC that the tradition tells of prophets in the southern kingdom of Judah. It was at that time and place that Isaiah and Micah lived and prophesied. Isaiah can be dated quite accurately by reference to contemporary political events. He was in evidence during the 'Syro-Ephraimitic war' of 733, when the Kings of Israel and Damascus tried jointly to force King Ahaz of Judah to take part in an anti-Assyrian coalition. Later, Isaiah went through the siege of Jerusalem by the Assyrian King Sennacherib in 701. The date of his call as a prophet is given in Isa. 6.1 as 'the year that King Uzziah died'; but that year cannot be determined with certainty.

Isaiah

When the prophets appeared on the scene, it was often in times when the people of Israel were in some special danger, in times of distress, particularly when they were menaced by more powerful enemies. For the country in which Israel lived was repeatedly exposed to the risk of being seized by the great powers, which wanted to expand their sphere of influence and ensure their predominance, and so tried to subjugate the small nations near them. For Israel, however, such menaces were not simply a matter of politics. Its history had always been understood from the very beginning as a history of God's dealings with his people – as a history of his continual guidance, but also of his abandoning them, as a punishment, to hostile powers. For that reason, times of severe strain in foreign affairs were always times of religious decisions, because they always involved Israel's relationship to its God. Time and again the prophets impressed this on the people, calling on them to make deliberate decisions in view of the previous history of their relationship to God, and to ask for guidance according to God's will at the existing moment of history. Thus the prophets, although they may be separated from each other by long intervals of time, form a continuous line. Their themes are very similar; yet each of the prophets has his own unmistakable individuality.

Among the eighth-century prophets Isaiah stands supreme. His special position is due only in part to the sheer volume of his prophecies that have been handed down to us. His words embrace an extraordinarily wide range of topics; and they show him to be an independent thinker, who often modifies and reformulates the traditional themes and ideas in a way that is all his own. We may, in fact, say that Isaiah is the theologian among

89

the prophets. He has also been called an aristocrat; and that is meant to stress on the one hand the fact that he was obviously born in Jerusalem and apparently belonged to the upper levels of society there, and on the other hand the loftiness and beauty of his speech, and the force and vividness of his images and similes. Isaiah's words form one of the peaks of Israelite prophecy.

How deeply Isaiah is rooted in the religious traditions of Jerusalem is shown very impressively in the magnificent vision, described in chapter 6, in which his call comes to him. In the Jerusalem temple there extends before him, in that vision, the background of the holy of holies, and he sees God himself on his throne, transcending the confines of the temple, which is filled even with the hem of his garment. And he sees the heavenly beings who surround the throne of God, and hears their hymn of praise: 'Holy, holy, holy is the Lord of hosts; the whole earth is full of his glory.' The boldness of the images, and the beauty and force of the language, make this passage one of the most impressive testimonies of visionary experience in the Old Testament. And it is also characteristic of Isaiah that he himself is drawn into what takes place in the vision; he hears a voice, and answers that he is ready to accept the mission with which he is charged: 'Here am I! Send me.' The whole of Isaiah's prophetic activity is coloured by the consciousness of that mission.

Jerusalem, too, is one of the main themes of his message. The historical situation very soon made it a matter of urgency, as the country and the city were menaced from without. In that moment of danger, with the hostile army approaching, he went to meet Ahaz and called on him to remain calm and trust in God's help for Jerusalem: 'If you will not believe, surely you shall not be established' (7.9) – in other words, 'If you do not trust, you will not be preserved.' Isaiah shows himself here as the guardian of a tradition that his contemporaries had forgotten. In former times Israel had repeatedly experienced God's help – in Moses' time when they were delivered from the Egyptian bondage, and frequently later in the time of the judges. Besides this, it was a conviction of long standing that Jerusalem, Zion, was under God's special protection. Isaiah called on the king to remember those fundamentals on which Israel had in past times built up its life. His political counsels have been described as utopian. But that kind of argument ignores the fact that in ancient times the direct historical puissance of the gods was thought to be a reality not inferior, but actually superior, to that of weapons. Isaiah, therefore, was not telling the king to choose between political realism and religious enthusiasm; on the contrary, he was asking him which reality he thought had the more weight – the power of Israel's God, or the troops of his Egyptian allies.

These verbal exchanges between prophet and king are in many respects characteristic. They show the opposition that so often came to the surface between religious tradition and reasons of state, as it had appeared as far back as the very beginning of the Israelite monarchy, between Samuel and Saul. They also show that as a rule, when the prophets urged people to remember the old traditional foundations, they could not carry their point. At the same time, it would be wrong simply to talk about the failure of the prophets' message. For the very fact that their words were written down and handed on shows that they were effective, in their own way, far beyond the particular moment of their utterance. The words of the prophets, and most of all, the words of Isaiah, have helped over and over again, throughout the generations and the centuries, to make people think back to the foundations of Israel's faith and thought.

That also holds good, in large measure, of another theme that occurs in Isaiah as in nearly all the prophets: the demand for social justice. Here, too, there was no innovation by the prophets, but a renewed and more vigorous assertion of a fundamental element in the Israelite tradition. On a previous occasion Elijah had confronted King Ahab when the latter tried to set aside the old Israelite agrarian law in favour of what the Canaanites regarded as the royal prerogative. But this was a development that had gained ground in Judah, too, in the course of time. The kings had distributed landed property on a large scale among their officials, and had thus thrown out of balance the traditional property-owning relationships. There had developed a regular speculation in land, and Isaiah denounced it in no uncertain terms: 'Woe to those who join house to house, who add field to field, until there is no more room, and you are made to dwell alone in the midst of the land' (5.8). In this matter, too, we can see his very positive interest in Jerusalem; he is lamenting that that city, which was once a stronghold of the law, has become an unfaithful harlot, to whom the law is now worth nothing.

However, he does not end on this note of accusation, but turns to the future; and that brings us to the last crucial element in his thought and message. However passionately he argues about the problems of his own time, and however hard he strives to bring about an immediate change of relationships, he also looks much further afield. He sees present events as parts of a great and far-reaching divine purpose in history. From the earliest beginnings God has been at work in the history of his people of Israel. And it is not only in the history of Israel, but also in the history of other nations, that God plans 'from afar', as Isaiah once puts it (10.3). And that plan reaches across the present and far into the future.

In all this, Isaiah, like many other prophets, sees the immediate future of his nation in anything but a rosy light. On the contrary, he proclaims the message that has been entrusted to him, that God's judgment on the nation is imminent, because it has again deviated from the way that was pointed out to it. But that judgment is not the last word. There will be a future in which a fresh start will be made. As with Elijah, there emerges here the idea of a 'remnant' that will form the basis for the nation of the future. Jerusalem will again be the city of the law, and in it there will be righteous judges as in former times. And above all, there will reign over the nation a king who, in contrast to those of the present time, will be entirely after God's heart, and will make law and justice a reality.

This resolute gaze into the future, with the expectation that God's action for the salvation of Israel and other nations still lies ahead, is the decisive contribution made by Isaiah and the other prophets of his time to the further course of the history of Israel and of mankind. Throughout the centuries that hope and expectation have continually supported new forces, which even today are working in many ways.

The emergence of the prophet Jeremiah is closely connected with the last phase of the history of the state of Judah. We are told in Jer. 1.2 that his activities began in the thirteenth year of the reign of King Josiah, namely 627 BC. It appears from the detailed accounts in the Book of Jeremiah that he was in Jerusalem during both the occupations (597 and 587), and that he was afterwards taken, against his will, by a band of refugees fleeing from the Babylonians to Egypt, where he was still active for a short time (chs. 43-44).

Jeremiah

Almost a century after Isaiah there appeared in Jerusalem another prophet, whose activity was to be of great significance for his contemporaries and for succeeding generations: Jeremiah. He was not, like Isaiah, born in Jerusalem; he came from the small country town of Anathoth, a few miles to the north. And he differs radically from Isaiah, not only in his origin, but also in his personality and circumstances as a whole.

What gives Jeremiah's work its own individual impress is, above all, his integral personal involvement in what he is commissioned to say and do – an involvement that often makes it apparent that his task causes him suffering. We can already see this in the account of his call in the first chapter of his book. Like other prophets, he told how he became a prophet: what happened to him was that he suddenly saw himself addressed and commissioned by God, and, one might say, hardly knew how it all came about. He himself describes his first shocked reaction: 'Ah, Lord God! Behold, I do not know how to speak, for I am only a youth.' But his protest is not accepted. God chooses his messengers himself, and he equips them so that they can carry out their mission; and so Jeremiah is promised that God himself will be with him and will put his words into his mouth.

Jeremiah applied himself to his mission. For several decades he faced his people with warnings and admonitions, as he had been told to. But again and again we hear how difficult it became for him, how he suffered under the burden of his office, how, in fact, he was sometimes in danger of collapsing under it. He felt himself shut out from the community of people round him, because he was constantly having to proclaim to them that God's judgment was at hand. And he expressed his laments in prayers that are among the most profound testimonies of human suffering and forlorn isolation: 'I did not sit in the company of merry-makers, nor did I rejoice; I sat alone, because thy hand was upon me, for thou hadst filled me with indignation' (15.17). Sometimes the lament even becomes an accusation: 'Woe is me, my mother, that you bore me, a man of strife and contention to the whole land! I have not lent, nor have I borrowed, yet all of them curse me' (15.10). And even God himself is accused: 'O Lord, thou hast deceived me, and I was deceived' (20.7). Here there are revealed depths of suffering that go almost beyond human limits. But again and again Jeremiah also tells how God gave him a helpful answer that made it possible for him to do and say what was entrusted to him.

Jeremiah's deep personal involvement in what he had to say and do is also shown in his representing the relationship between God and his people as a wholly personal, one might almost say an intimate one. He compares it to the relationship between man and wife, and he includes here not only marriage, but also the first youthful love. Thus in chapter 2 we read of God's saying to Israel: 'I remember the devotion of your youth, your love as a bride; how you followed me in the wilderness, in a land not sown.' The earliest period of Israel's history, spent in the steppe regions outside the cultivated land, is here described as the time of the first love. Israel did not hold to its first love; it did not keep faith, but turned to other gods. We meet here in Jeremiah a problem with which Elijah had had to deal more than two hundred years earlier – the worship of Canaanite gods. Even yet this question had not been finally disposed of, and again the prophet had to reproach the people of Israel with taking a wrong course, and call them back to their origins.

But the most difficult period of Jeremiah's life and work began when the Babylonian forces marched on his country to capture it. It was one of the critical phases of Israel's history when the existence of the little state of Judah, which was all that remained of David's glorious empire of former times, was threatened by superior hostile forces. Above all, there now arose the urgent question whether God would again on this occasion protect his city, as Isaiah and others before and after him had proclaimed that he would. Jeremiah's contemporaries believed that even in the present danger, the most desperate that had yet been experienced, they could cling firmly to that hope and the divine help. But again Jeremiah did not say what he was expected to say. He prophesied that the day of judgment on Judah and Jerusalem had now arrived, and that this time God would not protect his city; and he called on the inhabitants of Jerusalem to surrender to the Babylonians.

In this case Jeremiah had consciously broken with the tradition; and it was inevitable that he should be opposed by people who prophesied that this time, too, the city would be protected, and that there would soon be an end to the hostile menace. There now developed one of the most dramatic chapters in the history of Israelite prophecy. For the others, who pitted themselves against Jeremiah, claimed to be prophets and to speak in God's name; and so prophet spoke against prophet, word of God against word of God. We cannot now penetrate into the secret of how Jeremiah had reached his conviction. We do not know what part was played by his discernment of the international political situation, and how far it was direct divine revelation that made him so sure of his case. What happened within the mind and heart of the prophet is hidden from us; but as we read the texts, we can still feel the tremendous stress in which the whole affair must have been involved.

Jeremiah turned out to be right. But it is only too easy to understand that his contemporaries regarded him as a mischief-maker and defeatist. The situation is illuminated by a very interesting document that has come down to us from that period. Among the few Hebrew texts dating from the time of ancient Israel that have survived, apart from the Old Testament, there is a letter, found at ancient Lachish, (written, as was usual then, on a potsherd) saying that there were people in Jerusalem who 'weaken the hands of the country and city' – precisely the accusation recorded against Jeremiah in the Old Testament (Jer. 38.4). So we can see from that letter that the question disturbed people deeply enough for it to be talked about even outside Jerusalem.

And Jeremiah was persecuted and imprisoned, and was not set free till the victorious Babylonians marched in.

So things had taken the course that Jeremiah had foretold. Jerusalem had fallen, and Judah had finally lost its political independence and become a province within the great Babylonian empire. Many of the leading citizens of Judah and Jerusalem were deported to Babylon, as had happened for the first time ten years previously. But Jeremiah certainly did not regard that as the end of it all. He had seen God himself at work in the events that had taken place, and so now, even after the catastrophe, the history of God's dealings with his people was going on. In Jer. 29 there is a letter that Jeremiah wrote to the deportees in Babylon. It is an impressive indication of how he combined a sober and realistic view of the political situation with a strong hope for the future history of Israel as God's people. He warns the people living in exile not to harbour any illusions. He tries to prevent them from pinning their hopes on an early return, and so he urges them to adjust their lives as suitably and sensibly as they can to their existing situation. But he also tells them that one day, after seventy years, a new chapter in Israel's history will begin, and that the exiles will then go back to their own home, and there make a fresh start on the land that had been promised and given to their fathers. And he gives them a message from God: 'For I know the plans I have for you, says the Lord, plans for welfare and not for evil, to give you a future and a hope.'

That is what matters now – future and hope. Jeremiah turns his thoughts, as Isaiah did, more definitely towards the future, towards what God is planning for his people and for all peoples. But he, too, believes that, when the promised time of salvation comes, a new king, the Messiah, will appear and will rule over Israel under God's mandate.

It is specially noteworthy that Jeremiah also uses another word to express his expectation for the future: he proclaims that God will make a new covenant with his people. Here he takes up one of the weightiest ideas of Old Testament theology – the idea of the covenant. At all the decisive turning-points in the history of God's relation to Israel, the Old Testament speaks of a covenant: God made a covenant with Abraham, with Moses on Sinai, and then again with David; in fact, we read of a covenant made with Noah as soon as the flood was over, a covenant by which God undertook not to allow any new flood to come over the earth.

Here we can see plainly what is implied in the conclusion of these covenants. They are not a bilateral agreement between two partners of equal status; on the contrary, they contain a promise and an assumption of obligation by God; but at the same time they require of the human partner a fitting line of conduct. And therefore it is said again and again in the Old Testament that men have broken the covenant, and that by proving themselves unworthy they have put its continued existence in danger. But now (31.31-34) Jeremiah proclaims a new covenant, whose terms are written, not on ordinary writing material, but directly in men's hearts, so that it cannot again be broken.

Jeremiah recognized that men's relationship to God will constantly be in grave danger through their thinking that they can manage their affairs without him, through turning their thoughts to other things, and so forgetting to hold fast to the basis of their relationship. But he was very firmly convinced that, in spite of this, God would not abandon men, but would repeatedly turn to them again. He clothed that conviction in the words of the new covenant, which have since become one of the most momentous testimonies to the hope of a lasting and undisturbed relationship between God and mankind.

After the twofold deportation of sections of Judah's population in 597 and 587 BC, some of the Judeans lived in exile in Babylon. Their situation seems to have remained essentially unchanged for some decades. But from the middle of the sixth century new developments began to take place in the Babylonian empire. Under Cyrus the Persians broke away from Babylonian dominance, and quickly extended their power. In 546 Cyrus defeated King Croesus of Lydia, and in 539 he succeeded in capturing the city of Babylon, thus making himself master of the whole Babylonian empire.

It was in those unsettled years that there appeared the anonymous prophet whom we generally call Deutero-Isaiah, or the Second Isaiah. Cyrus is mentioned several times, but there is no clear reference to the capture of Babylon, so that Deutero-Isaiah may have died before then.

The Second Isaiah

In the decades after Jerusalem had twice been captured by Nebuchadnezzar, the exiles had to live in Babylon as captives in strange surroundings. According to the information that we have about their state, conditions seem to have been fairly tolerable; they could move about freely within a specified area, and in the main live their own life. At the same time, they naturally felt that their lot was a hard one. They had to live in a foreign country against their will; they had been wrenched away from their traditional way of life; and, above all, the foundations of the entire history of the nation seemed to have been wrecked. For in all periods of their history the people of Israel had regarded it as essentially a history of their relationship with God, or rather as a history of God's dealings with his people. From the very beginnings in the times of the patriarchs, and then of Moses and David, it had been a history of God's guidance; and in spite of many dangers and afflictions that the people had had to endure, they had always been certain, in the long run, of God's help. Now, all that seemed to be over; the firm promises under which the people had seen their history seemed to be no longer valid. Many wondered whether God had abandoned his people and would no longer help them. Some went further, and asked whether God *could* still help them. For it was precisely because the people's history was so intimately bound up with God's guidance that they felt there was no option but to regard the Babylonians' victory as a victory of the Babylonian gods over the God of Israel. Were they perhaps really stronger than he? Was he really the great and only God, greater than all others, as they had hitherto believed and confessed?

Those doubts and questions were bound to occupy the minds

of the exiles, and to make their situation, which was already outwardly bad enough, still more difficult through such inward conflicts. But in that situation, too, there were prophets to raise their voices, offering explanation and help, but also admonitions and warnings. The Old Testament tradition tells us of two prophets in particular. One is Ezekiel, who combines in a peculiar way prophetic and priestly characteristics. He takes up a good deal of what the earlier prophets had said, and carries it over into the changed situation. In this he is particularly concerned with the question whether God is present with his people now in a foreign land just as much as he was in their homeland, where his presence was felt, above all, in the temple at Jerusalem. After a strange vision in which he sees God present but veiled in a dazzling blaze of light, Ezekiel proclaims that God has left Jerusalem in order to be with his people in exile as long as the captivity lasts. He is therefore concerned that the exiles should not feel that they are excluded from everything that their history, their relationship with God, and the experience of his presence in their midst, has so far meant to them. Through this, Ezekiel undoubtedly made an important contribution to maintaining the continuity of Israel's history over the decades of the exile.

There is another prophet whose influence was even more important. He occupies a unique place in the history of prophecy, for we know nothing about the outward circumstances of his life; in fact, we do not even know his name. When the prophetic utterances were collected in books, what was recorded of him was added to the Book of Isaiah, where it now forms chs. 40-55. So, as he is anonymous to us, we call him the Second Isaiah (or, using a foreign word, Deutero-Isaiah). His words are among the most impressive and beautiful in the Old Testament; and many of them are familiar to Christians and are often used in our church services. 'Fear not' is one of his sayings that we come across repeatedly, and the comforting 'I have redeemed you; . . . you are mine.'

Although we do not know who this prophet was, his words give us a penetrating view of the Israelites' situation in the Babylonian exile. For what he says is directly related to his fellow captives' questions and problems, which he either answers or puts in their proper form. So, for instance: 'But Zion said, "The Lord has forsaken me, my Lord has forgotten me"' (49.14). Or, 'Why do you say, O Jacob, and speak, O Israel, "My way is hid from the Lord, and my right is disregarded by my God"?' (40.27). Here we can see right into what the exiles were discussing: God has abandoned and forgotten us; our fate no longer interests him.

But the way in which the prophet now takes up these questions is most striking; he reminds the Israelites of what they had formerly believed and confessed in their homeland: 'Have you not known? Have you not heard? The Lord is the everlasting God, the Creator of the ends of the earth. He does not faint or grow weary, his understanding is unsearchable.' It almost sounds as if the answer were a quotation, perhaps taken from the hymns that had been used in worship at Jerusalem and were therefore known to every Israelite. What Deutero-Isaiah says here and in many other passages could well be in the Psalms, where some of those hymns used in the services are collected. This kind of answer, however, is characteristic of this prophet. He does not want to supply the questioners and doubters with cut and dried answers from without, but rather, one might say, to convince them from within. He tries to reawaken the living memories that they themselves have from their services and from Israel's religious tradition; he recalls to their minds their own and the nation's experiences of their history and their relationship with God; he makes it clear to them that, in the last resort, they themselves know where they stand. For indeed, what they are saying cannot be true. God cannot abandon them, any more than a mother can abandon her child. The tie between God and his people is much too intimate to be loosened, let alone destroyed, by the events of the recent past.

This intimate relationship of God to his people is repeatedly expressed by Deutero-Isaiah in God's messages, which are formulated in the most personal terms: 'Fear not, for I have redeemed you; I have called you by name, you are mine' (43.1). The direct explicitness of the language is meant to restore to the exiled Israelites the certainty that God is near, to help and comfort them. And we read again and again that God will redeem and rescue his people. For in all this the point is not merely that the exiles are to be comforted and reconciled to their fate. This prophet, like the others, is most firmly convinced that God's relationship to Israel is conclusively expressed in his historical actions. Just as throughout past times God has dealt with Israel during its history, so he will now continue to act.

In concrete terms, that means that the prophet is telling his fellow captives that one day their captivity will come to an end, and that God will bring them back to their homeland, the land of their fathers. To describe that return he uses bold images, in which a miraculous divine intervention changes the pathless mountain wastes that now lie between the exiles and their homeland into a fertile countryside that can be easily crossed: 'Every valley shall be lifted up, and every mountain and hill be made low; the uneven ground shall become level, and the rough places a plain' (40.4). And God will make 'rivers in the desert' (43.19), so that those who have to cross it will not die of thirst. This is the prophet's answer to his fellow countrymen's doubting questions as to how such a return could ever be possible in view of their immense distance from the motherland, and the almost unimaginable difficulties of the journey. He is firmly convinced that God's purpose will not be frustrated by these difficulties.

That conviction is based on the certainty that the God whom Israel has experienced in its history, and whom it acknowledges, is the true and only God. That question, which had become so problematic for many of the exiled Israelites, is at the very centre of Deutero-Isaiah's thinking and of his prophetic proclamations. And here his argument is comprehensive. The ultimate proof that God is the true and only God is the fact that it is he who created the world. This article of faith was one of those with which all Israelites had been familiar ever since their childhood, and which took a prominent place in the hymns and psalms which were part of their worship. 'The Lord is the everlasting God, the Creator of the ends of the earth.' God's creative activity is referred to in vivid pictures: he 'stretches out the heavens like a curtain, and spreads them like a tent to dwell in'; and his supreme greatness is expressed in such passages as 'Who has measured the waters in the hollow of his hand and marked off the heavens with a span, enclosed the dust of the earth in a measure and weighed the mountains in scales and the hills in a balance.'

For the exiled Israelites, God's supreme greatness and power has a twofold significance. First, it strengthens their own hope and confidence: the God who possesses such power, and has shown it time and again ever since the creation, will also have the power now to free his people from their captivity and take them back to their homeland. Secondly, this power of God at the same time precludes the claims of all other gods and powers. Only one is the Creator, and therefore only one is the real Power, and only one is the true God. So the same words, which bring comfort and encouragement to the captive, take on an almost harsh and polemic tone. 'I am the Lord' – that means on the one hand comforting and helping: 'I am the Lord, your Creator and Redeemer, who will help you.' But on the other hand it may mean 'I am the Lord, and there is no other. There is no other god besides me. The other gods are nothing; they are the creation of human hands, and they have no power.' And the prophet can pour scorn on people who worship such gods made with hands.

So this prophet combines, in a most impressive way, the acknowledgment of the God who is the only true God with the certainty that this God is constantly turning to his people to help and comfort them. And it is this God who created the world, and who directs the destinies of mankind from its very beginnings. In his hands, too, is the future of his people and of the whole world. And so with this prophet, as with others before him, the vital thing is the view of the future. He still expects something from God. He expects that there will be another fresh start in his people's history, and that there will again be a history of God in his dealings with his people. But at the same time he looks out, beyond the boundaries of his own people, on the history of all mankind, which will be drawn into the orbit of God's actions.

This unknown prophet helped substantially to enable the people of Israel to endure the grievous years of the Babylonian captivity, and actually one day to make a fresh start. To be sure, this new beginning was not as wonderful and glorious as Deutero-Isaiah had indicated. But it was the beginning of a new epoch in Israel's history, an epoch that was to be of world-wide significance.

With the capture of Babylon by the Persian King Cyrus, a new period began in the history of the Near East. After Cyrus' son Cambyses had subjugated Egypt in 525 BC, the Persians were for the next two centuries masters of a greater empire than any yet known. For the history of Israel, Cyrus' religious edict of 538, which made it possible to rebuild the temple, was of great importance. Later Artaxerxes I (465-424) supported the rebuilding of Jerusalem by sending Nehemiah there. The Persian king who sent Ezra to Jerusalem was also named Artaxerxes. According to the present arrangement of the various accounts in the Books of Ezra and Nehemiah, Ezra appears as a contemporary of Nehemiah. But there is a good deal to be said for giving his activities a later date and connecting them with Artaxerxes II (404-359).

Ezra and Nehemiah

With the end of Babylon's world domination, a new period began in Israel's history; for the Persians' policy towards their subject races was different from that of the Babylonians. They took pains to maintain peace and quietness in their domains by granting their subject races a large measure of autonomy. In particular, they allowed them their independence and freedom in the religious sphere; and so, in many cases, they restored what the Babylonians had destroyed.

Thus, one of the first measures taken by the government of Cyrus, the new king of Persia, was to give permission for the wrecked temple in Jerusalem to be rebuilt. Even the actual wording of the royal decree has been preserved for us in the Old Testament, in Ezra 6. It is evident from this how handsomely Cyrus behaved; he not only gave permission for the rebuilding, but he ordered at the same time that the expenses were to be paid out of the royal treasury. And he also ordered that the gold and silver vessels that Nebuchadnezzar had taken to Babylon from the temple should be returned. Now, after more than half a century, a fresh start could be made in Jerusalem.

The start was, indeed, slow and hesitating. There was severe and widespread destruction, there was great poverty, and great despondency among the Israelites. It was only by degrees that more energy was infused into the work by those who returned from Babylon, first with the temple vessels, and then in gradually increasing numbers, to the land of their fathers, and brought with them the will to reconstruction. And once more it was the prophets who supplied the essential contribution which made the progress of the historical development possible. The prophets Haggai and Zechariah did not cease to encourage and admonish their compatriots in the work of rebuilding the temple, and to strengthen their hopes of a better future. It was undoubtedly due in part to their efforts that the work was at last finished, even though on a modest scale. In 515 BC, a little more than twenty years after Cyrus' decree, the new temple could be dedicated.

This meant that Israel again had a religious and intellectual centre. It is true that the country was part of a Persian province and had no political independence; but it was now possible for Jerusalem and the rest of the land of Judah to develop a new life of its own. Outwardly, of course, things were still wretched enough. The rebuilding of the city was a slow business; the city walls were still in ruins, and the inhabitants had not the means to rebuild them unaided. What was needed to bring about a change was a fresh impetus from outside, from among the Israelites living in Persia outside the motherland.

That impetus came from a man who had risen to a position of some esteem in the Persian court, his office being that of the king's cupbearer. His name was Nehemiah. Reports had come to him of the state of affairs in Jerusalem, and he resolved to make an effort to help the city of his fathers. He succeeded in getting the necessary authority from the Persian king, and so he went to Jerusalem with a military escort. In the report drawn up by himself and handed down to us in the Old Testament, he describes the difficult and sometimes dramatic conditions in which he had to set about his work and carry it through. For to the internal problems of Jerusalem and Judah there were added external difficulties, in particular from the neighbours in the immediate north, the Samaritans. The leading inhabitants of the territory of the former northern kingdom of Israel, with its capital Samaria, were foreigners, settled there by the Assyrians some centuries before, and this had caused a radical division between the two parts of the country, especially in religious matters. This was made more acute by the fact that the Persian governor who was responsible for the whole territory had his headquarters in Samaria, so that the revival of Jerusalem was necessarily seen there as unwelcome competition.

But Nehemiah succeeded in gaining the co-operation of the country's inhabitants as a whole. Working together, and in spite of the impediments and threats that came from Samaria, they performed the astonishing feat of rebuilding the city walls of Jerusalem, and their gates, within two months. They were dedicated at a great celebration. It meant an important step forward, for now Jerusalem could increasingly take over the role of capital for the whole territory of the former state of Judah. And it was obvious to everyone that by sending Nehemiah the Persian king was allowing Judah the status of an independent province, and so Nehemiah was able to become its first governor.

Politically, that small remnant of the former Israel could play no more than a modest part. But it formed the necessary basis on which the traditions that had been handed down through the long centuries of its history could again find a focal point where they could be cultivated and become the foundation of further history. This development was further promoted by another impetus that came from the Diaspora.

Among the Israelite exiles in Babylon there was a priest named Ezra. He evidently had some official position, and his title, translated literally, means 'Writer of the law of the God of heaven'. That denotes a definite official rank, and it might be rendered approximately as 'Adviser on Israelite religious affairs'.

This Ezra was sent to Jerusalem by the Persian court on an official errand. It seems to have been a matter of putting into force in the province of Judah certain religious regulations, the absence of which was felt, as time went on, to leave a gap. Their central point was the 'law of the God of heaven', as the official Persian title reads. It is not quite certain what is meant by this law; but in the main it probably coincided with the first five books of the Bible, which the tradition calls the 'Five Books of Moses'. Ezra's essential task was to promulgate the law in due form, and to have it put into force.

We find in the Old Testament an account of how Ezra formally and solemnly read out this law and laid the whole people under an obligation to keep it. That was an act of fundamental importance for the whole future history of Israel and Judaism. For it was here that the traditions of the Israelite religion were for the first time written down and made the basis of the community's life. It was the first step in the formation of the 'canon', the authoritative collection of Holy Scripture that finally became the 'Bible'. Although it was to be centuries before all the writings that today form the Jewish Bible and the first part of the Christian Bible, the 'Old Testament', were collected and recognized as the Holy Scriptures, the foundation of that development was now laid by Ezra.

Of course, the proclamation of the 'law' did not mean that something completely new had happened. On the contrary, it had been an essential part of the Israelite religion from the earliest times that certain laws and regulations for the community were regarded as obligatory. In the course of the centuries, they had been collected and written down and linked with the name of Moses; and so here the Ezra narrative refers explicitly to the 'law of Moses'. The new factor was that all the laws were now collected and written down in a form that was to remain unchanged in times to come. This decisively strengthened the 'Torah', the 'instruction', as a standardizing and directing force.

It would, however, be one-sided if we were to look at all this simply from the point of view of the development of Judaism into a 'religion of the law', as we often say. The establishment of the Holy Scriptures as having binding force had other and quite different results. Thus, it was of very great importance that these writings could become the connecting link between the Israelites – or the Jews, as we shall in future call them – all over the world. For after the time of the Babylonian exile many Jews lived outside their motherland. Their numbers rose constantly, and the development of international trade and communications involved their settling in more and more countries of the world as then known. They were certainly acutely conscious everywhere of belonging to the land of their fathers and of their association with the long history of their nation. That consciousness was now given a vital support by these writings, which not only set out the laws, but also contained an account of the beginnings of Israel's history. And so it was no accident that the first translation of these scriptures soon appeared in Greek, which was then the ordinary colloquial language of the Mediterranean world. For many Jews who lived outside their original homeland soon adopted the language of their surroundings. But now these scriptures gave them a connecting link with their own origins and with other members of their nation. Finally, the place that the Bible has attained in the Christian religion would be unthinkable but for these beginnings. For the collection of writings that began here was the first Christian 'Bible', and it was only gradually that there were added the Christian writings proper, which were then collected in the 'New Testament'.

Ezra's work, then, was of quite exceptional importance for the whole future. On the one hand, it completed, in a way, the work initiated by Nehemiah in the consolidation of Jerusalem and Judah, both outwardly and inwardly; and on the other hand it created at the same time the conditions that made it possible for Judaism, in its world-wide dispersion, to maintain its inner cohesion. In that twofold aspect of Ezra's work we can already trace the basic elements that characterize the whole future of Judaism. For in the many centuries that have come and gone since then, the Jews throughout the world have always felt that the part played by the ties with the land of their fathers, and especially with Jerusalem, was fundamental, even in times during which physical contact was hardly possible. And wherever they lived, and whatever language they spoke, they have always found their common spiritual and religious focal point in the Book of the Torah.

And the Christians, who later took over this book from the Jews, and share it with them to this day, have always had, and still maintain in many ways an interest in the laying of this two-fold foundation.

The psalms that have come down to us in the Old Testament cover a period of many centuries. The oldest poems go back to the time before the monarchy, as for example the 'Song of Deborah' (Judges 5), which was composed after the battle with the Canaanites in the twelfth or eleventh century BC.

Many psalms reflect the public worship in Jerusalem during the monarchy, whereas others obviously contain references to the destruction of Jerusalem in 587, or to the state of the exiles in Babylon. There are also some that date from the post-exilic period.

The Psalmists

The figures that go to make up our picture of the Old Testament do not consist merely of the men and women whose names we know, and whose words or deeds have been preserved for us in the tradition. There is also a group of people whose names we do not know, and who have yet made a very important contribution to the influence that the Old Testament has exercised through the centuries on countless men and women. They are those, often unnamed, who composed the Psalms, which for the Christian as well as the Jewish religion have become one of the most vital parts of the Old Testament.

At first sight it might seem as if we were well informed about the authors of a large part of the Book of Psalms. Almost half of the one hundred and fifty psalms that have been collected there mention at the beginning the name of David; and attached to some of the others we find other names, among them Moses and Solomon. But here it is probably not, in most cases, a question of giving the actual author. Even the linguistic form of these introductory notes leaves open the possibility of different interpretations. Besides the usual translation 'A Psalm of David', it is also possible to understand the Hebrew text as meaning 'for David'. It is also open to question whether this means David himself, or simply the king who was sitting on David's throne in Jerusalem. And lastly, we must suppose that many things in the tradition were made to converge on David, a figure that became of such significance as an example to later generations – just as the great number of laws that also originated in later times were associated with the name of Moses.

For the image of David as the singer and poet was firmly anchored in the tradition, and formed a strange contrast to his reputation as warrior and statesman. Thus we already read in the stories about him at the court of King Saul that he could play a stringed instrument, and that he could use it to drive away the 'evil spirit' that plagued the king. And on occasion the stories about him contain psalm-like songs that he is supposed to have sung, and probably composed too: for example, the moving lament on the death of King Saul, and two songs at the end of the story of his life. So it is quite possible that some psalms do go back directly or indirectly to David; but many of those that bear his name show clearly the characteristics of a later time, or refer to later events, so that they must have been written by other people.

Among the names at the beginning of the various psalms we find some that give us interesting and valuable indications as to what kind of people wrote them. A number of them are associated with a man named Asaph, and those of another group mention at the beginning the 'Sons of Korah'. Both these names are to be found in the Books of Chronicles among the temple singers who were responsible for the liturgical singing in the temple of Jerusalem. So the people with whom those particular psalms are connected might be called the official 'church musicians'.

In point of fact, many of the psalms have the unmistakable imprint of formal public worship; and that means that psalms were certainly composed before the building of the temple in Jerusalem. One of the oldest psalm-like passages in the Old Testament is, no doubt, that short song that, according to Exodus 15, was sung by Moses' and Aaron's sister Miriam over their pursuers after the deliverance of the Israelites from the Egyptians: 'Sing to the Lord, for he has triumphed gloriously; the horse and his rider he has thrown into the sea.' That little song, which according to its form can almost be called a psalm, probably had its place in a service of worship and thanksgiving for the deliverance that had been experienced. And later on, for similar reasons, it was expanded into a full-sized psalm which was, as it were, developed from that little song and now stands just before it in the same chapter.

We have here an interesting glimpse into the history of the

psalms. A particular event would be the direct occasion of the composition of a short song, which was often repeated later, and then expanded for the solemn public worship on feast days, perhaps in the temple at Jerusalem. That meant that the composer did not confine himself to the event in question, but went far beyond it in praise of God's saving acts that had taken place during Israel's history.

Another psalm-like song, which has also come down to us outside the Book of Psalms, bears directly on an occasion in the early history of Israel. One of the most important events in the history of the Israelite tribes before the monarchy was the great battle that they had to fight against a coalition of Canaanite kings in the Plain of Jezreel in the northern part of the country. In Judges 5 we have a song of triumph celebrating the successful issue of the fight, the 'Song of Deborah'. Here, too, a prominent feature is the glorification of the mighty God who saved his people from the danger of defeat; but at the same time the poet, who seems to have been an eye-witness of events, gives a very vivid account of the fight, in language of great poetic force and archaic beauty.

A number of other psalms, too, recall historical events; but it is often not easy to fit them very accurately into their contexts in point of time. For the psalmists look rather at the basic experiences that are repeatedly confirmed in new ways by individual events. Thus, many psalms that speak of God's actions in history do not mention actual events as such, but rather trace, in a connected historical sketch, the way in which God has led his people Israel. In this the writers often show themselves to be not only poets who are masters of linguistic expression, but also theologians who set out Israel's religious experiences in a striking way.

At the same time, the psalmists were not entirely free in their choice of linguistic devices and of the form in which they presented their message. For psalms were, in fact, a definite and fixed part of the divine service, and so there was always a specific framework into which the psalm had to fit. It was a component part of the liturgy, and it may be that some of the psalms, in which we can detect a change of persons and themes, themselves represent entire liturgies of certain feasts or parts of feasts. But the very fact that the poets were tied to that religious framework must make us admire even more the variety of ways that they found to express the basic experiences and perceptions of the Israelite religion.

The praise of God's actions in history constantly formed the basis of the liturgical poems for the great festivals. But a whole series of psalms goes beyond this, and extends its scope to another great realm in which God's power is to be seen – the realm of creation. Here we can follow another line that was of some importance in the history of psalm-composition in Israel. A number of the psalms that sing of God's actions in creation show clear traces of a tradition that goes a long way back; they speak of God in a way that was probably common among the Canaanites, who had lived in the country before the Israelites, and to some extent continued to live there alongside them. Indeed, David had adopted in Jerusalem certain existing elements of the Canaanite royal cult; and so it is not surprising that here and in other places other features of the Canaanite religion also found entry into Israelite religion and worship.

Some of the most beautiful psalms that sing of the creation give a clear indication of their affinity with non-Israelite poetry. In Psalm 19, for instance, we read that 'the heavens are telling the glory of God'; and we read of the sun 'which comes forth like a bridegroom', and, like a strong man, runs its victorious course in heaven. The sun almost seems here to be regarded as a god; in any case it is given a place that it did not otherwise have in Israelite thought. Another psalm (29) speaks of the phenomenon of God's power as it expresses itself in thunderstorms. This psalm is of great poetic beauty and expressiveness; but it speaks of God quite differently from the other psalms, which take Israel's historical traditions as their basis. Again, another psalm (104), which praises God's power in the creation of the world, uses pictures that remind us of other nations' mythical traditions about the creation of the world, saying that in the beginning the chaotic waters covered the earth, but that they fled before God's voice, that they had to release the earth from their power, and that God then 'set a bound which they should not pass'. This suggests a struggle of the Creator against the hostile forces of chaos, as they are described in the myths of other ancient oriental religions. The same psalm then describes the complete order and harmony that rule in the creation, and in that respect reminds one quite clearly of certain Egyptian hymns that have come down to us.

So we see that the psalmists of Israel learnt a great deal from other nations. They may even have adopted the most important artistic rules of religious poetry after they had immigrated into the land of the Canaanites. But at the same time these psalms also show the poetic and theological strength with which they brought these elements of foreign origin into the framework of the Israelite religion and its literature. For although research has made clear the Canaanite roots of these psalms, or of certain elements in them, yet for the Israelites in Old Testament times they were an established part of the Israelite religious tradition, as they are for the Bible-reader of today.

Besides this, certain psalms that have as their theme the special position of Yahweh, the God of Israel, show this process of appropriation and adaptation. They speak of God as king: 'The Lord is king.' That means primarily that he is king over the gods. Israel's neighbours supposed that there were many gods, one of whom was their king. There was certainly never any such pantheon in the Israelite religion; but in order to assert God's supremacy in relation to the gods of other nations, they used that idea and incorporated it in their own religious poetry. The psalms did not speak of Yahweh as king of the gods; they regarded his kingdom as a sovereignty over mankind, and especially as a kingdom over Israel. Indeed, the psalmist can finally call God 'My King', and so once more give the whole thing a different sound.

Thus the psalmists played an important part in the history of Israelite religion. Of course, we cannot now lay down in detail how far they strengthened existing insights, or co-operated in the development of new perceptions. In any case, their poetry is likely to have contributed greatly to the general religious consciousness. For it was constantly being sung at worship, possibly by temple choirs, whom the congregation would answer with a refrain or an 'Amen'. In this way everyone was familiar with it, and many Israelites probably found in these hymns the best way of expressing their faith.

But it was not merely the joyful and uplifting aspect of Israel's experiences that were expressed by the psalmists; they also uttered lament, and prayer for help and deliverance. Some of these psalms of lament reveal dire distress or menace facing the whole nation. In such times special services were held, which were associated with fasting and in which God's help was besought; and here, too, it was the psalmists who gave the expression to the feelings of all the people. Among the psalms of lament we find not only some that are simply concerned with present distress, but others which, in a similar situation, look rather to the long history of Israel's experience of God. In the afflictions that visited the people, they recognized the consequence of having repeatedly taken a wrong course; and the praise of God's actions in history suddenly become a lament and an accusation about the backsliding that had so often occurred throughout that history, whose other aspect was now seen as a calamitous record of Israel's defection from the foundations of its faith, and of chastisement inflicted by God. And that backward look at their history gave rise to the petition, not only that God would help the people out of their present distress, but that he would lead them back to the right way and would graciously accept their contrition.

Thus the psalmists also rendered a valuable service to their nation in such times of distress. They opened its eyes to the situation as it really was, and called on the people to see and repent. And furthermore, even in the most grievous times, they expressed the common feeling, when Jerusalem and the temple were destroyed and part of the nation was sent into exile. There is evidence of this in a whole series of lamentations that the later tradition associated with the prophet Jeremiah. And even among those who were sent into exile, who, in the words of Psalm 137, 'by the waters of Babylon . . . sat down and wept', there were poets who put into words their anguish and grief.

Besides the psalms that we can see were used on many and varied occasions of public worship, there are others that express the quite personal problems of individuals. Although these do not find a place in the regular festivals and services of the whole community, they are not merely personal prayers spoken by the individual privately on his own account; for even the lament and thanks of the individual were voiced by prayer in the temple or in some other sanctuary. There is an excellent example of this in the account of the birth of Samuel, at the beginning of I Samuel. His mother Hannah, who was childless, had uttered a prayer of lament in the temple at Shiloh, and Eli the priest had promised her that her petition should be granted. Then, when her son was born, she again came to the temple to give thanks to God and to fulfil the vow that she had previously made, that she would dedicate the boy to service at the sanctuary. She expressed her thanks in a psalm; and we see here how, in the temple, individual Israelites repeatedly voiced lament and petition on the one hand, and praise and thanks on the other, using psalms as their means of expression.

We do not know who composed these psalms; but some of the authors will certainly have been in the ranks of the temple-singers. For when an Israelite went to the temple to give vent to his feelings of distress or joy, he was not often likely to be in a position to compose for himself his laments and petitions, or his thanks, in the form of a psalm. But there were set prayers ready to hand, and new ones were constantly being added, so that he would be able, in one or other of them, to express his feelings. We can illustrate the connections between the personal situation and the set prayer by the hymn-books that we find in use among Protestants. The hymns they contain are often used to express quite individual and personal concerns. And although the passages, taken in detail, do not always exactly correspond to the particular situation of the person who is praying, yet they may well include his particular concern and serve to express his thoughts. He can, as it were, find shelter, with all his troubles, in the familiar lines of the hymn-book, and get support from them.

Here again, the psalmists deserve our admiration. For although they are concerned with prayers for general and everyday use, they have nevertheless used them to portray all the heights and depths of human destiny. The deepest distress and loneliness, even as far as the almost despairing question of Psalm 22, 'My God, my God, why hast thou forsaken me?', find expression here, as does the absolute certainty of God's faithfulness. And they continually reflect the many occasions that might lead people to utter their laments and petitions in the temple. The psalmists also knew the intimate connection between sorrow and sin. In not a few of the songs of lament it is stressed that what the petitioner is asking God to do is not only to help him out of his present distress, but, in the last resort, to forgive him his guilt and restore him in mercy. And almost every theme that is suggested in the songs of lament has its counterpart in the songs of thanksgiving, so that the petitioner could resume the thread of his prayer when, after his distress or grief had been overcome, he came into the temple to give thanks to God and to perform – generally by a sacrifice – the vow that he had made in his lament.

So the psalmists, more than almost anyone else, gave expression to the piety of the individual Israelite; but it is certain, too, that through their poems they left their own mark on that piety, and helped to shape it. And particularly for the further historical influence of the Old Testament, the importance of their songs and prayers can hardly be overestimated. One might say that the Jewish prayer-book lives on the Psalms, and many of the prayers that were composed later and have found their way into it are clearly indebted to the piety and the language of the Psalms. For Christian worship, too, the Psalms have acquired a fundamental importance. From the very first they have formed an important part of the liturgy, and in Protestant worship many of them have been given a new life through being rewritten as hymns. Although we do not know the psalmists' names, their songs and prayers live on in many different forms.

In the ancient East there was a lively interchange of cultural ideas between the different countries and cultural regions; and so Israel, too, shared early in the civilization of other countries. That included, among other things, the cultivation and handing on of the traditions of 'wisdom' that had been developing since the time of Solomon, with some dependence on foreign models, especially Egyptian ones. The lines of thought and the stylistic forms of wisdom are to be found in many types of Israelite literature in the succeeding centuries. In the post-exilic period wisdom-poetry again flourished in Israel; but at the same time arguments arose about wisdom's basic ideas; and these are reflected in, for instance, the Books of Job and Ecclesiastes.

Job

Old Testament thought is primarily about history; God's actions in the history of the people of Israel and in the history of all mankind are the real theme of a large part of the Old Testament writings. Beside that, there is a second theme, which also lies at the basis of biblical thought – the law. It accompanies, so to speak, the first theme from the beginning; the first basic legislation reported in the Old Testament, for the people of Israel, was promulgated through Moses, who stands at the very beginning of Israel's history; and the line is continued as far as Ezra, who, long after the Babylonian captivity, put the people under an obligation to observe the written law, and so laid the foundations for further history.

But beside history and law, there is yet another kind of thought in the Old Testament: as early as in the tradition about King Solomon we read of his 'wisdom'. This 'wisdom'-thought was widespread throughout the ancient East, and it was also cultivated in Israel. It included the most diverse subjects: the pattern of nature; corporate life in one's family and tribe or at the royal court; and lastly, man's relation to God. This wisdom-thought is reflected in various books of the Old Testament: particularly in the so-called 'Proverbs of Solomon', but also in certain of the Psalms and other writings. In all these writings the author's concern is to comprehend things in their order and harmony, to trace the laws governing the world's phenomena, including the relationship between God and man.

But the Old Testament has preserved texts which show that this self-contained awareness of the order of things did not always remain untroubled and undisputed. We find evidences of a deep-seated doubt as to a divine world-order, or perhaps of

125

a doubt as to whether it can be discerned. Any such doubt might find expression in very different ways. Thus, in Ecclesiastes there is a thorough-going scepticism about everything that wisdom teaches. 'All is vanity' says the sceptic; what is the use of all the trouble that a man takes, and above all, what is the use of his uprightness and wisdom? His destiny overtakes him all the same, and the fate of the wise man is no better than that of the fool. But the preacher does not revolt, nor does he cast doubt on the divine ordering of things. He keeps within the limits of Old Testament ideas with regard to faith, but he gives up the possibility of making them a coherent whole.

In the Book of Job we meet an entirely different kind of doubt. Things are seen from a different angle, with heights and depths experienced to a degree that is almost unique in the Old Testament. Job shakes the foundation pillars of the Old Testament's traditional beliefs.

Of course, it is not easy to get a comprehensive and understanding view of such a unique and sublime work. First of all, it is clear that it consists of two entirely different parts joined together. The framework is a narrative – certainly a very old one – of a pious man named Job, whose piety is put to the test with divine approval. And in spite of all the suffering imposed on him, which he cannot understand, he holds fast to his faith.

This narrative, which is essentially plain but impressive, is in sharp contrast to the rest of the book, which records vigorous dialogue, the product of the most profound intellectual and theological reflexion. Job and his friends persistently reformulate their approach in discussing the problems of human life and man's position before God. In these dialogues, Job's questions and doubts are often of breathtaking boldness, and not seldom they come close to accusing and challenging God.

But surprisingly, one cannot discover any progressive line of thought in these dialogues. Again and again the argument is renewed, and the rejoinders are often anything but answers. Each participant looks at the problem in his own way, and it often seems as if he simply had not heard the other man's arguments. They talk round the problem, so to speak, and examine it from all sides, in trying to find a solution.

The occasion of the problem is Job's suffering. In ancient times suffering was thought to be directly connected with man's actions and conduct: an evil deed is followed necessarily and inevitably by an evil destiny. In the Old Testament, too, we often find in different forms this idea of the deed that shapes the destiny; one may put it by saying that the deed recoils on to the head of the doer. And so, conversely, the prevailing view gave rise to the conclusion that anyone who suffers has sinned. For, according to that way of looking at it, any suffering that befalls a man must be the consequence of an evil deed. How else could it occur? This thought is closely related to what we have called wisdom-thought, for we are dealing here with a ruling order that carries within itself its own logic and inevitability.

But Job cannot allow that these assertions are valid. He has fallen into suffering, but he is not aware of any sin that might be the reason for it. His friends persistently urge him to recognize the connection, and to confess his guilt before God. But Job refuses. He calls on his friends to show him his guilt of which he knows nothing; indeed, he calls on God himself to tell him why he is so obviously angry with him. Again and again, with stronger and stronger expressions, he persists in asserting his uprightness and in demanding justice. He calls on God to have the legal issue between them cleared up in a court of law.

For us Christians today Job's attitude is difficult to understand; for behind it there is an understanding of righteousness that does not at once tally with ours. For Israelite thought, righteousness is not, in the first place, a matter of individual conduct; its essential basis is not primarily what this or that person does or does not do. Righteousness before God has its basic root in the relationship of the covenant that exists between God and the people of Israel. As long as Israel stands in that covenant, as long as it 'lives up to it', it is righteous before God. And in that case, the individual Israelite shares in that righteousness. That is why he can so passionately insist on his righteousness, because he is conscious of having a claim to it.

But at the same time, the attitude of Job and his friends shows that that way of thinking had reached a crisis, increasingly so as the thought turned on the individual person. For as far as the fate of the individual was concerned, that understanding of righteousness given by God through the covenant could no longer be readily accepted; in any case, it could not cover all the ranges and aspects of individual destiny. So Job's basic problem is the individualizing of a faith that is at present regarded as a matter for the community as a whole rather than for the individual.

The peculiar difficulty of the problem here is that Job himself can think of no other answer; he has nothing to offer in place of the conventional view. All that he can do is to realize and experience most acutely for himself that that view is no longer adequate to solve the problems of the faithful individual who suffers. But his own questions do not go beyond its confines. His grave doubts as to the adequacy of the old ideas never enable him to break through them and produce new ones in their place.

Above all, Job is anything but an atheist. On the contrary, he makes the most desperate efforts to clarify his relationship to God; he tries to understand God's actions, and is profoundly grieved that he fails to do so. In consequence, he is dragged from one extreme to the other. In his despair, he sometimes sees God as a downright enemy who is doing his utmost to destroy him. But after such outbursts of horror at that God he again uses quite different language expressing profound trust, saying that he is sure of safety in God even on the other side of death: 'I know that my Redeemer lives' (19.25), and 'Even now, behold, my witness is in heaven' (16.19).

But even these expressions of trust do not solve the problem. Again and again Job comes back to it; his questions and doubts are not silenced, and his friends' answers have long since ceased to touch his questions. Finally the solution of the problem comes in an entirely different way. After they have all finished their speeches, there begins something quite new: Job receives a direct answer from God. At the end of the long dialogues there is a long speech from God to Job.

But when we look at this speech, we realize that it does not really answer Job's questions at all; it seems to be dealing with quite different things. And Job suddenly sees himself as the person who is being questioned, but on a completely different plane from that on which he himself had conducted the discussion. 'Where were you when I laid the foundations of the earth?' is the first question addressed to him; and it is one that made it clear to him very bluntly that he had been putting his questions on much too low a level. For there now follows a lofty description of God's creative activity, dealing with things that lie far outside Job's field of vision – with the stars, the deepest depths of the sea, the origins of light and darkness, and the laws that the seasons obey. But the speech also deals with what happens on earth, with things that do not touch mankind and are yet part of the work of creation: the life of animals in remote parts of the world, inaccessible to man, also has its place, just as man himself has, in creation as a whole.

And Job realizes and admits that his questions were quite out of place; and he puts his hand on his mouth, so as not to begin them again. He admits that he has been talking about things that are far beyond his power of comprehension; indeed, he confesses to God: 'I had heard of thee by the hearing of the ear, but now my eye sees thee.' He has been given a glimpse of a world that is quite outside his range, and he realizes that that glimpse has upset his standards, and that God cannot be measured with the yardstick that is provided by the world of human life and experience.

This solution may seem to us unsatisfactory, for the difficult questions about guilt and man's destiny, which are stated so dramatically in the dialogues, do indeed remain unanswered. And the question of God's justice also remains unanswered – at least in the form in which it was put. But the answer that the Book of Job gives is nevertheless most impressive. For it puts man's life and its problems into a much larger setting. It makes it clear how inadequate it is for man to try to measure and evaluate God's actions on the basis of the little segment of reality that he can see. It is an answer that makes him small before the greatness of the creation and the Creator – not to humiliate him, but to enable him to realize his place in the whole of this great structure. And this is certainly one answer to man's questions – not the only answer or the ultimate one, but still an answer that he must not leave out of account if he wants to avoid running the risk of making himself the centre of the world and of judging the things about him by inadequate standards.

After the end of the state of Judah in 587 BC, part of the Jewish people lived outside their original homeland, in the Diaspora or Dispersion, especially in the wide tracts of the Persian world-empire. They seem to have lived there, in the main, unmolested, apart from occasional conflicts such as are recounted in the Book of Esther and in the stories about martyrs in the Book of Daniel.

The history of the great Persian empire drew to an end when in 333 Alexander the Great had won his decisive victory over the Persians. After his death and the protracted struggles that followed, the empire was divided among the 'Diadochi' or 'successors'. At first the Ptolemies, who were ruling in Egypt, succeeded in bringing the Jewish territory under their domination. But about a century later, in 198, the Seleucids, who were ruling in Syria, were able to extend their rule further to the south and annex the territory. Under the Seleucid King Antiochus IV (Epiphanes) there were severe struggles between the Jews and their foreign overlords, which are reflected in the visions related in the Book of Daniel.

Daniel

Since the time of the Babylonian exile part of the Jewish people
had been living outside their own country, in the Diaspora. For
not nearly all those who had been deported by the Babylonians
returned later to their homeland; and in other countries, too,
there lived Jews who had gone there at widely different times.
Pieces of evidence, both direct and indirect, have come down to
us in the Old Testament about life in the Diaspora; and one of
them is the Book of Daniel.

The narratives about Daniel and his friends give us an insight
into the situation of certain circles of Diaspora Judaism. They
show us that members of those circles could rise to high office
at foreign courts, as was the case with Nehemiah and Ezra. At
the same time they make us realize what problems could arise
there.

The foreign rulers' attitude towards Daniel and his friends
seems at first to be a genuinely positive one, and the latter, for
their part, show themselves to be loyal citizens and officials of
the foreign state. But then situations arise that produce conflict:
the Jewish food laws make it impossible for Daniel and his
friends to eat the foods provided from the royal kitchen. They
refuse to worship the king's statue, and, although they are
threatened with the severest penalties, they will not discontinue
their prayers to the God of Israel. So they find themselves in the
greatest peril: they are condemned to the cruel ancient forms of
capital punishment – to be burnt alive and to be thrown into the
den of lions. But they are rescued in a miraculous way from such
an extremity, so that finally the foreign king himself acknowledges the superior power of the God of Israel.

We can regard these narratives of Daniel and his friends as

stories of martyrs; for these men suffer for their faith. But at the same time it is evident that the stories are to be thought of as representative in character. Their principal aim is not to describe particular events and fortunes, but to provide example and instruction for Jews living in foreign surroundings. Their intention is to show how the very fact of living in close association with an environment based on a different faith can suddenly produce situations in which loyalty to the faith of one's fathers may be put to severe test. In effect, they call on people to be vigilant, and they admonish them not to fall into disloyalty, however great the danger. And at the same time, they show them that God does not leave his own people in the lurch. That does not mean that they indulge in a naïve faith that expects a miraculous rescue as a matter of course. On the contrary, Daniel and his friends reckon all the time with the possibility of their not being rescued, as they clearly indicate to the king (3.18): 'But if (our God will) not (deliver us), be it known to you, O king, that we will not serve your gods or worship the golden image which you have set up.' Cheerful confidence *and* readiness to suffer − these stories about martyrs are a call to both.

The historical setting given in these narratives puts them as early as the time of the Babylonian King Nebuchadnezzar and soon after. But there is a good deal to be said for making the period a later one, as their background is the situation of Jewry in the Persian Diaspora, where there was obviously a comparatively quiet and peaceful coexistence for a fairly long time, but where sudden conflicts might yet break out again.

Who Daniel, the chief hero of the narratives, really was, we do not know. Noah, Daniel, and Job are named in the Book of Ezekiel (14.14, 20) as three men of exemplary righteousness, and one has the impression that all three may figure in a very old tradition. And outside the Old Testament the name Dan'el has been handed down in a mythical text from the Phoenician port of Ugarit. It is likely enough that the authors of these stories of martyrs used such well-known names for stories meant to serve as examples.

But the picture of Daniel has at the same time other and quite different features. In the narratives in the first part of the Book of Daniel he is already showing his worth as the interpreter of the king's dreams and ominous visions. This feature becomes more pronounced in what follows: Daniel is shown to us as a seer to whom God reveals, in various visions, the connection of historical events in the past, present, and future.

Here the supreme question is one of ultimate world-domination. This has already been referred to in ch. 2, in King Nebuchadnezzar's famous dream about the colossus with feet of clay, which Daniel interprets to him. One world-empire will supersede another, each being inferior to the preceding one – from the head of gold down to the feet which are partly of iron and partly of clay. But they are all swept away by a new empire which, like a stone without the help of human hands, will crush everything and then will itself fill the earth. Human empires are therefore approaching their end, and will be superseded by a new and ultimate empire, established by God himself.

The same expectation is shown in Daniel's vision of the four beasts in ch. 7. Here again, one world-empire follows another, each more terrible than the one before, till at last their place is taken by a new and ultimate empire. Then there emerges a mysterious figure, of whom it is said: 'And behold, with the clouds of heaven there came one like a son of man. . . .', and to this son of man 'was given dominion and glory and kingdom, that all peoples . . . should serve him.'

In Hebrew and Aramaic, the expression 'son of man' means in the first place simply the individual person as distinct from the generic notion 'man'; and so in this connection it expresses the idea that now, after the world-empires symbolized by animals, the empire of man is dawning. This man is the divinely appointed ruler of the last days; and in this there is a clear connection with the expectation of the Messiah, as we find it in the prophets.

Thus Daniel with his visions continues, in a way, the expectations of the prophets. But at the same time there are deep-seated differences. The prophets were primarily concerned with the

135

history of the people of Israel; and although they repeatedly looked out beyond it, yet for them the salvation of the nations was mediated through Israel. For Daniel, however, the historical horizon has again greatly widened. It is now a matter of world history as a whole, which is embraced in a grand view of universal history. World-empires come and go, and God's all-embracing historical purpose rules over all.

In this, Daniel is one of the first representatives of a new movement that arose in Jewish thought during the last centuries before Christ. We generally describe it as 'apocalyptic', from the Greek word *apokalypsis* which means 'revelation'. In the apocalyptic writings many diverse elements of the Israelite tradition have been combined afresh: on the one hand prophecy with its orientation towards the future and the expectation of a final time of salvation brought in by God; on the other hand wisdom with its efforts to understand the relationships of natural phenomena and the laws and ordinances to which they are subject. To these were added various ideas from the Hellenistic and Iranian environment, which had become widespread throughout the Near East during those centuries.

This new line of thought is determined, above all, by the expectation that the end of the present world-order is close at hand. The apocalyptic writers see themselves at the turning-point of the ages. The present world is destined to pass away, and a new world of the future is already approaching. Contemporary thought was therefore deeply influenced by tense expectation of the great turning-point that was believed to be imminent.

But it is not to be a matter of just sitting back and watching the events that are taking shape. On the contrary, the apocalyptic writers do their best to see right into what is happening in all its contexts; for they are deeply convinced that what is now happening is an essential part of a great divine historical purpose. And that again introduces something new – an investigation of the traditional writings, to find out what references they contain to that divine purpose. So Daniel applies himself to the question what is meant by the seventy years which, according to the prophet Jeremiah, are to pass over the ruins of Jerusalem. And the explanation that comes to him is that they mean 'seventy weeks of years' (9.24), i.e. seven times seventy years, and that therefore the turning-point that Jeremiah had announced is now close at hand.

That interpretation is given to Daniel by an angel. Here, too, is a characteristic feature of the new line of thought: the idea of angels and other beings in the intermediate sphere between God and man becomes more and more prominent. It is the angels who initiate man into the mysteries of the divine historical purpose, and it is they who wage the final battle against the satanic powers that still stand in the way of the realization of God's kingdom. They sometimes appear as clearly identifiable figures who are called by name. Thus Daniel gets his revelation through the angel Gabriel; and the name of the angel Michael, 'the great prince', makes its first appearance in the Book of Daniel.

What gave the Book of Daniel its special importance was that it appeared at a time of great suffering and distress, when the Jews were engaged in desperate struggles against excessive and brutal domination by foreign overlords. It was very helpful and strengthening at that time to have contemporary events put into a wider context. Those who were being cruelly oppressed received the assurance that they did not stand alone in the fight against superior forces, but that their struggle was part of a great final dénouement under God's historical purpose, which determined in the last resort, through the powers under his authority, the issue of the fight.

But the Book of Daniel has also had a marked effect beyond its immediate contemporary importance. For not only was the apocalyptic literature that was now developing vitally influenced by this first work, but more than that, for many centuries, and even into modern times, writers who have tried to give an overall view of world history have repeatedly turned to the model of the four world-empires as traced in the Book of Daniel.

Many of the ideas and thoughts of the book must seem strange to us today under changed conditions. But for that very reason it is important that we should try to understand it in the context of its own time. We cannot reach a genuine understanding of the texts of bygone times unless we are prepared to make allowances for their different character and perhaps their strangeness, and not to take them at the face value which they have for us, thus judging them over-hastily. We shall then often see that the texts' importance for us is much greater, although mediated indirectly, than we had at first supposed. They have entered into the thought of the centuries and have helped to shape it, and so they have become part of our own intellectual pre-history. For that reason the Book of Daniel is one of the important books of world literature, because it has produced lasting and far-reaching effects.

In 175 BC Antiochus IV ('Epiphanes') mounted the throne of the Seleucid empire. During his rule, trouble leading to bloodshed developed in Jerusalem and in the whole of Judea. It began in 169, when he plundered the treasure in the Jerusalem temple, and it reached its climax in 167, after he had instituted pagan rites in the temple. The Maccabees rose against him, and in 164 they were able to restore the temple worship.

The Maccabees, who were also called the Hasmoneans, also succeeded, for the first time for more than four hundred years, in again setting up a Jewish state with limited political independence; and from about 100 BC they had the title of king. After long years of struggle the Hasmonean kingdom ended with the accession of Herod in 37 BC.

The Maccabees

The change from the rule of the Ptolemies to that of the Seleucids was of great importance for the situation of Judaism; for it meant that the Greek outlook and practices found their way increasingly into almost all spheres of life. It was the time of 'Hellenism', when the Greek mind penetrated the whole world of the Near and Middle East, and, for its part, was changed through meeting the eastern mind. In the Old Testament those impacts have left comparatively few traces, for by that time the greater part of the Old Testament writings had already been completed, and only some of the later works, as, for instance, the Book of Daniel, are contemporary with them. But we learn something about the period, which was so momentous for Judaism, from various writings which may in a wider sense be regarded as part of the Old Testament, and in particular from the Books of the Maccabees. They are not in the official Jewish canon of Holy Scriptures, but they find a place in the Septuagint (the Greek translation of the Old Testament), from which they have been taken into the official Latin Bible of the Roman Catholic Church. In the Protestant Churches they have not been included in the Bible proper; but Luther included them, together with other writings, under the term 'Apocrypha' in his translation of the Bible.

The Books of the Maccabees show us something of the problems caused by the impact of the Greek mind on Judaism. First there were inward tensions between those who held fast to the inherited traditions that were based on the Torah, and others who were willing to accept Greek customs and ways of living. These tensions were expressed in disputes about the setting up of a 'gymnasium', a place for games in the Greek style, where the physical education of youth would be carried on and competitions staged. At first sight, this seems merely to be a question of the pattern of living, a dispute between progressives and conservatives. But the problems lay deeper. The athletic competitions of the Graeco-Hellenist world were closely connected with the cults of certain gods; and therefore to set up a gymnasium would be at the same time to allow entrance, in some measure, to the worship of strange gods. So one can understand that many Jews saw this as gross offence against the foundations of their faith, and one in which they could not and would not acquiesce.

What made the problems still more acute was that politics and religion were closely bound up together. For the direction of the Jewish community was at that time in the hands of the council of elders, presided over by whoever was high priest at the time. That meant that the highest religious and the highest political office were identical. That, in its turn, meant that the questions of religious policy, which at the same time involved the attitude towards the Hellenist rulers, were bound to arise in connection with the appointments to this office, and that this led, on occasion, to sharp clashes.

Finally, however, it was the Seleucid ruler himself whose conduct brought the matter to a head. It was King Antiochus IV (Epiphanes) who interfered grossly in the religious life of the Jewish community. Hungry for power, always needing money for his widespread campaigns, he did not shrink from plundering the treasure in the Jerusalem temple, this being, no doubt, in line with his previous actions in other parts of his empire. In this case he even violated the holy of holies, which only the high priest, once a year, was allowed to enter. It was an action that aroused extreme indignation among the Jews who were devoted to the law.

All these things led to an insurrection in Jerusalem. Antiochus crushed it mercilessly, and as a counter-measure he set up in the city, which had been partially destroyed, a citadel occupied by inhabitants who were submissive to him. To strike at the roots of the religious resistance, he had the worship of the Greek god Zeus introduced into the temple, and prohibited all Jewish religious practices: the offering of sacrifices, the observing of the sabbath, and the circumcising of newly-born boys were forbidden on pain of death, the rolls of the Torah were confiscated, and in the townships outside Jerusalem the people were called on to take part in pagan sacrifices. But for many Jews who were devoted to the law, this finally went beyond what they were prepared to put up with.

The revolt flared up first in a small Jewish town. When a royal official appeared there and summoned the people to participate in the pagan sacrifice, the head of a family from the priestly line of the Hasmoneans came out against him and struck him dead. This was the signal for open revolt, which soon took the form of organized military resistance, with one of the sons of the rebellious priest assuming command. His name was Judas, and he was nicknamed Maccabeus, which probably means 'the hammer'. We are told (in I Macc. 3.4) that 'he was like a lion in his deeds, like a lion's cub roaring for prey'; and he does, in fact, seem to have been a man of exceptional energy and high courage. More and more Jews gathered round him to fight the foreign ruler, and they were surprisingly successful. Judas Maccabeus and his followers succeeded in defeating the hostile troops several times, and soon he had wrested the greater part of the Jewish territory from the Seleucid domination.

But the insurgents' decisive aim was bound to be the restoration of worship in the temple at Jerusalem; and in this, too, they succeeded. In 164 BC, three years after the desecration of the sanctuary, the temple precincts were again in their hands, and they were able to take steps to cleanse it from all foreign elements, and to restore their own worship as laid down in the Torah. The temple was rededicated with a great festival lasting a week; and every year since then the Jews throughout the world have celebrated the event in the festival of Hanukkah.

Although the struggle was not yet finally over, the decisive step had been taken. The Jews had regained their religious independence, and a little later they were granted a limited political independence under their own monarchy, which remained for more than a century in the family of the Hasmoneans or Maccabees.

The years of the Maccabean revolt were decisive in more than one respect. Never before had the question of holding fast to the traditions of the fathers involved such a severe crisis. Never had the external and internal dangers threatening the Israelite-Jewish religion been so great, and never had such a measure of readiness to sacrifice and suffer been demanded from those who were determined to stand fast. If we want to understand what sources of strength made that readiness possible, we have to take into account the whole intellectual and religious background of the time. We can get a good idea of this in certain Old Testament writings, and it is particularly clear in the Book of Daniel. In it a series of martyr-stories tell us of the steadfastness of Daniel and his friends, who ran the most deadly risks by refusing to abandon the faith of their fathers, and were finally saved in a miraculous way. There is no doubt that such narratives helped to strengthen the courage and steadfastness of those who were hard pressed because of their devotion to the law.

Another aspect of the Book of Daniel is relevant here. In it the visions of Daniel the seer give us a picture of world history as a great series of connected events directed by God; and it is evident that Daniel, like many of his contemporaries, was convinced that the end of that world history was close at hand, and that God would soon bring in his final empire of salvation and peace. The Maccabees and their supporters were also inspired by the same consciousness that they were involved in a great final struggle for divine world domination against all the opposing forces. That consciousness gave them strength to perform their valiant deeds.

Although the expectation of an immediate end of that era was not fulfilled, it would be impossible to overestimate the importance of the Maccabees' struggle for the future of Judaism. In a time of the utmost peril, forces had been awakened which were often tested anew during the coming centuries. Again and again there came times of oppression and persecution, and again and again it was not least the Maccebees' example that strengthened the oppressed people and gave them fresh courage.

In all this it is certainly not primarily the military achievements that deserve the highest place of honour. Even more important, the Maccabees and their supporters provide us with an early example of the conviction that the religious tradition, the inheritance from the fathers, contains values for whose preservation no risk is too great. They showed that, in times of crisis, life is not the ultimate and highest good that is worth fighting for, and that there are things that alone make life worth living, and whose abandonment deprives life itself of its meaning. Since their time, Jews in all parts of the world have often been faced with the question whether, for the sake of self-preservation, they would abandon their Judaism, or whether they would rather give up life itself. And there have always been some for whom life was not the ultimate thing or the highest. They took as their example the attitude of Daniel and his friends who in Maccabean times had already shown the way: 'But if (our God will) not (deliver us), be it known to you, O king, that we will not serve your gods . . .'

But it was not only for Jews that the crucial foundations were laid here. A few centuries later the first Christians in the Roman empire were often in a similar situation to that of the Jews at the time of the Maccabees and later. And the first Christian martyrs were, in a way, in the succession of the Jews of Maccabean times, who had suffered and died for their faith.

One of the darkest chapters in the history of Christianity is that later on, after that early common experience of suffering, it was often the Christians from whom the Jews had to fear persecution and death. Attempts to compel them to abandon the foundations of their existence – that is, of their faith – now came often enough not from the pagan, but from the Christian powers. Instead of community and comradeship through faith in the one God, there now often prevailed hostility and hatred.

Perhaps, at a time when the relationship between Christians and Jews is being thought out afresh, some contribution might come from their looking back together to the first martyrs, the Jews of Maccabean times. Of course, we shall have to take care not to make the Maccabees an object of hero-worship. But we can learn from them, even today, that for Jews and Christians alike there is an obligation to obey God, the God to whom they both owe allegiance, rather than men.

Herod, although an exceptionally ambitious and unscrupulous ruler, was also very energetic and successful. He was responsible for a good deal of building activity, traces of which still remain. After his death in 4 BC, the territory that he had ruled was divided, Galilee, in the north of the country, being given to Herod Antipas, who is simply called 'Herod' in the New Testament, and who ruled till AD 39. Other parts of the country, including Judea, were given to Archelaus, who was deposed by the Romans a few years later. His territory was put under Roman government, and one of the Roman procurators was Pontius Pilate.

It was during this time that Jesus of Nazareth appeared. We cannot give the exact dates of his life and work, as the supposed year of his birth, and therefore of the Christian era, was not officially settled till later. But Pilate's tenure of office from AD 26 to 36 gives the dates within which Jesus' crucifixion must have taken place; many scholars now think the date was 7 April in the year 30.

With the destruction of Jerusalem and the temple by the Romans in the year 70, and the crushing of the rebellion led by Simon Bar-Cochba in 135, Jewish political history ended for the time being.

After the Old Testament

From the patriarchs Abraham, Isaac, and Jacob, through the kings and prophets, to Daniel and the Maccabees – the history spanned by the Old Testament covers much more than a thousand years. But it is not a history that is finished, sealed, and stowed away in archives. For the fact that we are still concerned with it means that it has continued to take its course and to exercise its influence.

With Daniel a new phase of Jewish thought was initiated, a period of the most intense expectation that the end of the present imperfect temporal era, and the beginning of the final reign of God, were imminent. Not only did that movement give rise to an extensive literature, but there also repeatedly emerged individual figures who voiced the expectation of that time in a particularly impressive way, and so collected a great many people round them. One of them was John who was called 'the Baptist'. He must have made a great impact on his contemporaries, for we are told that many came to him, and Mark (1.5) even says that 'all the country of Judea' went out to him at the river Jordan. There he proclaimed the approaching end of the existing era, an end that would culminate in an all-embracing judgment from which no one – not even the people of Israel – would be exempt.

At that time there were also other groups of people who held that all Israel had defected from God. Just at the northern end of the Dead Sea there lived on monastic lines a community whose writings have come to light again within the last twenty years or so. Its members, too, were firmly convinced that Israel would not escape the final judgment. They therefore withdrew from the rest of the people and formed a kind of sect with which they believed that God had made a special covenant, so that all who joined it in faith would be preserved from the judgment.

But John did not invite people to join a sect. Standing at the busy trade route that crossed one of the fords of the Jordan, he preached for everyone to hear. He proclaimed to all and sundry the possibility of being saved, through repentance and conversion, from the final judgment; and as a sign that conversion had taken place, he baptized in the Jordan those who were ready to repent, so as symbolically to wash away their sins.

With his proclamation of judgment and his call to repentance, John was in the succession of the prophets of earlier centuries; they, too, had repeatedly proclaimed God's judgment and called the people to repentance. But he combined in a special way the tradition of the prophets with the proclamation of the imminent last judgment. It could be said of him that he was 'more than a prophet'; both he and his disciples felt that he stood at the turning-point of the ages.

Among those whom John baptized was Jesus of Nazareth. He may possibly have belonged for a time to John's band of disciples. Later, when John had been killed by Herod, Jesus himself continued John's preaching about the approaching judgment and the dawning of God's reign. His activity was carried on in the first place within the Jewish world and in the setting of its history. Although he cannot be compared with any other figure in Israelite-Jewish history, he yet belongs to it; and it must be emphasized that his coming and his message can be understood only against the background of that history.

At the same time, however, he was introducing something new. He claimed that the dawning of God's reign was involved in his own coming, and that men's attitude towards him would decide who was to be saved from the final judgment. And he took a further step beyond John, not only by regarding everyone as sinners and liable to judgment, and by calling them to repentance, but also by offering salvation to sinners in particular. That meant turning accepted standards upside down. His consciousness of standing at the turning-point of the ages was so deep-rooted that the existing standards were no longer valid for that hour of decision.

It was inevitable that Jesus' pronouncements should give rise to violent disputes. Opinion on him was divided; he had supporters and resolute opponents. The rift widened when the Romans condemned him to death by crucifixion as an agitator, and when, a few days later, his supporters announced that he had risen and was alive. These soon formed a community of their own, united in the belief that in him there had really dawned the new long-awaited final era. At first his new community was nothing more than a small group inside contemporary Judaism; and it was only gradually that it grew increasingly out of its Jewish environment, and with that there began a new period – the history of Christianity.

That brought to an end the period of the Old Testament and its immediate sequel. The continuation of that history takes two separate courses. There is a further Jewish history, which extends over the whole world and regards itself as a direct continuation of Old Testament history. But beside this there is a history of Christianity, which also stands in the succession of Old Testament history. Both are inseparable from their Old Testament origin, without which, indeed, both are quite unthinkable.

The fact of their being deeply rooted in Old Testament history is what inseparably links Judaism and Christianity together. But it not only links them together; it has also, in the course of history, repeatedly pushed them apart. In particular, the attitude of the Christian world to the Old Testament and to Jewish history has undergone great changes in the course of the centuries. It may perhaps be said to run a course between two opposite extremes.

On the one hand, voices have repeatedly been raised from within Christianity, demanding a complete and radical separation from the Old Testament and the history of Israel. They would not recognize the existence of a positive connection between the Christian faith and that of the Jews as expressed in the Old Testament; and they saw in Christianity a radical contrast to everything that had gone before it. As early as the second century AD the demand was voiced that the Old Testament should be eliminated from the Christian Bible; and the demand has been put forward again and again, right down to our own days. But that would mean tearing up the roots from which Christianity has grown, and without which it would certainly wither. If we tried to talk about Jesus while ignoring his connection with the history of Israel, he would become a mythical figure that had originated somewhere in man's imagination without regard to historical facts. And if we tried to talk about God without thinking of him as the Creator and Lord of history according to the evidence of the Old Testament, we should have to withdraw into mere inward contemplation, and leave the world and history to themselves. Christianity without the Old Testament would be nothing more than its own shadow.

This attitude is matched by the other extreme, which regards the Christian Church as the sole legitimate owner of the Old Testament, and denies that the Jews still have the right to lay claim to it. It regards the Christian community as the 'true Israel', and as the sole heir to the Old Testament promises. In support of this view, it appeals to the apostle Paul, who distinguishes between an 'Israel after the flesh' and an 'Israel after the spirit'. But the same Paul expressly emphasized (Rom. 11) that the rise of a Christian community did not mean the annulment of God's promises to Israel: 'I ask, then, has God rejected his people? By no means! I myself am an Israelite, a descendant of Abraham, a member of the tribe of Benjamin. God has not rejected his people whom he foreknew.'

This view – that the Old Testament belongs solely to the Christians – is basically, though perhaps unconsciously, due to an assumption that Judaism really cannot and ought not to have existed since the beginning of Christian history. The horrible consequences that this way of thinking has had in our recent history stare us all in the face. And it is important that we should realize that this refusal to admit a legitimate Jewish continuation of Old Testament history is one of the root causes of the relationship between Christian and Jews, and therefore of the terrible history of the Jewish people's sufferings.

For it can hardly be imagined that Christians would behave as they have so often behaved towards the Jews, if they realized the depth of the common roots of Judaism and Christianity in the Old Testament and its history. Judaism and Christianity have a common root. In other words, Jews and Christians are brothers, sons of the same father. Brothers, it is true, who have gone separate ways through many centuries, brothers who will never hold identical views on every question of their faith and life; but brothers who, if they will consider afresh the common roots of their faith, can go on their way harmoniously together.

In recent decades, we Christians have learnt better than before that the various Christian confessions, in spite of all the things that separate them, are interdependent and must go on their way together. Our next step must be to learn that the same thing applies to our relationship to the Jews. For nearly two thousand years the things that separate us have had the upper hand. The time is now ripe for us to consider again the things that link Judaism and Christianity together: their common roots deep down in the Old Testament and its history.

CHRONOLOGICAL TABLE

About the middle of the second millennium BC	The patriarchs
About the mid-thirteenth century	Exodus from Egypt Moses
About the thirteenth to twelfth centuries	Settlement of the Israelite tribes Joshua Samuel
About 1000 BC	Establishment of the monarchy Saul David Solomon (to 926)
926	Separation of Israel and Judah

ISRAEL			JUDAH		
926-907	Jeroboam I		926-910	Rehoboam	
882-871	Omri				
871-852	Ahab	Elijah			
		Elisha	851-45	Jehoram	
845-818	Jehu		(845-840	Athaliah)	
841	Jehu pays tribute to Shalmaneser III		840-801	Joash	
787-747	Jeroboam II	Amos			
		Hosea	742-725	Ahaz	Isaiah

733 Syro-Ephraemite War

ISRAEL		JUDAH		
721	End of the state of Israel	725-697	Hezekiah	Micah
		701	Siege of Jerusalem by Sennacherib	
		639-609	Josiah	Jeremiah
		587	End of the state of Judah	Ezekiel
			Babylonian Exile	Second Isaiah

539	Conquest of Babylon by Cyrus	
515	Rebuilding of the Temple Completion of this (Ezra?)	Haggai Zechariah

445 ff	Nehemiah in Jerusalem (Ezra?)
323-198	Judea under the rule of the Ptolemies
From 198	Judea under the rule of the Seleucids
175-163	Antiochus IV 'Epiphanes'
167	Desecration of the temple Maccabean revolt
164	Re-establishment of worship in the temple
About 140-37	Rule of the Hasmoneans
37-4	Herod the Great
AD 26-36	Pontius Pilate Procurator of Judea John the Baptist
About 30	Crucifixion of Jesus
70	Destruction of Jerusalem by the Romans
132-135	Jewish revolt under Bar-Kochba

FOR FURTHER READING

John Bright, A History of Israel, Westminster Press, 1959; SCM Press, 1960

Walther Eichrodt, Theology of the Old Testament, translated by J. A. Baker, SCM Press and Westminster Press, Vol. I, 1961, Vol. II, 1967

Curt Kuhl, The Old Testament. Its Origins and Composition, translated by C. T. M. Herriott, Oliver and Boyd and John Knox Press, 1961

Martin Noth, The History of Israel, 2nd edition of the English translation, revised by P. R. Ackroyd, A. and C. Black, 1960

John H. Otwell, A New Approach to the Old Testament, SCM Press and Abington Press, 1967

Gerhard von Rad, The Message of the Prophets, translated by D. M. G. Stalker, SCM Press, 1968